In Praise of Mary

veritas

Donal Flanagan

In Praise of Mary

Veritas Publications Dublin 1975

First published 1975 by
Veritas Publications,
Pranstown House, Booterstown Avenue, Co. Dublin.

©1975 Donal Flanagan

Typography by Liam Miller
Cover by Steven Hope
Set in 11 pt Baskerville by Mary Neenan
Printed and bound in the Republic of Ireland by
Cahill and Co., Limited, Dublin.

Nihil Obstat:
Richard Sherry, D.D.

Imprimi potest:
+ Dermot,
Archbishop of Dublin.
May 1st 1975.

The Nihil Obstat and Imprimatur are a declaration that a
text is considered to be free of doctrinal or moral error.
They do not necessarily imply agreement with opinions
expressed by the author.

The author and publishers are obliged to the following:
Éditions Universitaires, Fribourg, Suisse, for permission
to quote from The Acathistos Hymn.
Darton, Longman and Todd Ltd for permission to quote
from Vatican II, Lumen Gentium.
Penguin Books Ltd for permission to quote from
The Prayers and Meditations of Saint Anselm, trans.
Sister Benedicta Ward.

ISBN 0-901810-80-0
Cat. No 3312

Contents

PART 1 THE MARIAN TRADITION
Introduction   9
1 From East to West   21
2 From the edge of the world   27
3 They called her "Our Lady"   32
4 No false praise   39
5 An Age of Mary?   55
6 Paul VI: To honour Mary   69

PART 2 SELECTIONS FROM MARIAN LITERATURE
Hymn of praise (Akathistos hymn)   82
Latin hymns to Mary   96
The poems of Blathmac   99
Anselm: Prayers to St Mary   104
St Bernard: Sermon on Luke 1:26-27   114
Dante: The Divine Comedy   116
From the writings of Martin Luther   118
From the Colloquy of Erasmus   121
Pius IX: Ineffabilis Deus   126
Pius XII: Mystici Corporis Christi   129
The Legionary Promise   131
Vatican II: Lumen Gentium   134
Paul VI: Marialis Cultus   147

Suggested further reading   173

PART 1
THE MARIAN TRADITION

INTRODUCTION

Born of a woman *(Gal 4:4)*

God is not the God of Christians only but the God and Father of all men. When he sent his Son, Jesus, it was to be the Saviour of *all* men. St Paul writes in his letter to the Galatians:

> When the fulness of time was come God sent his Son, born under the law that we might receive the adoption of sons *(Gal 4:4)*.

We were all to be sons adopted by God. God's Son was sent to be "the first born of many brothers" *(Rom 8:29)*. The human family can see in Jesus its destiny. All are called to be children of the one Father, the Father of our Lord Jesus Christ. All are made to become brothers and sisters of Jesus, to share his inheritance.

Paul notes that Jesus came among us "born of a woman". Christians from the very earliest times have understood that this most special woman, the Mother of Jesus, has an interest not only in the Son of her flesh, but in all those who are called to be his brothers and sisters. Already

in the early years of Christianity we find a prayer
we still use today:

> We fly to thy patronage, O holy Mother of God;
> despise not our prayers in our necessities, but ever
> deliver us from all dangers, O glorious and blessed
> virgin.

This prayer which now introduces the Litany
of Loreto shows that in their troubles Christians
fifteen hundred years ago approached the
Mother of God with confidence. When, therefore,
the second Vatican Council refers to Mary as
Mother of God and Mother of men it is not
putting forward some new teaching. It is saying
something which has been in the heart of the
Church and in the hearts of Christians for a very
long time:

> Let the entire body of the faithful pour forth persever-
> ing prayer to the Mother of God and *Mother of men.*
> Let them implore that she who aided the beginnings
> of the Church by her prayers may now, exalted as she
> is in heaven above all the saints and angels, intercede
> with her Son in the fellowship of all the saints. May
> she do so until *all the peoples of the human family,*
> whether they are honoured with the name of
> Christian or whether they still do not know their
> Saviour, are happily gathered together in peace and
> harmony into the one people of God for the glory
> of the Most Holy and Undivided Trinity.

If we look back over the history of the Church
and of Christian devotion to the Mother of God
we must be struck by its continuity, its variety
and its sincerity. The words of our Lady in the
Magnificat have indeed come true: "For behold,
henceforth all generations will call me blessed."

My soul proclaims the greatness of the Lord,
my spirit rejoices in God my Saviour;
for he has looked with favour on his lowly servant,
and from this day all generations will call me blessed.

The Almighty has done great things for me:
holy is his Name.
He has mercy on those who fear him
in every generation.

He has shown the strength of his arm,
he has scattered the proud in their conceit.
He has cast down the mighty from their thrones,
and has lifted up the lowly.
He has filled the hungry with good things,
and has sent the rich away empty.

He has come to the help of his servant Israel,
for he has remembered his promise of mercy:
the promise he made to our fathers,
to Abraham and his children for ever.

History has not belied these words, for as
Christianity spread, new people accepted Christ
as their Saviour and the praise of his Mother was
sung in new languages down through the centuries.

All generations

"Hail, full of grace, the Lord is with you.
Blessed are you among all women and blessed is the
fruit of your womb" *(Lk 1:28).*

These words of Gabriel are the earliest words
of praise addressed to our Lady and those which
set the pattern according to which generation after
generation of Christians will speak to her. In long

prayers or in short prayers, in private prayers or
in public liturgical veneration this basic theme
will be found. Mary will be hailed as "full of
grace" and as "blessed among women".

The early Christian centuries show us examples
of prayers and sermons in praise of Mary, and
also some very beautiful poetry in her honour.
Thus the fifth-century Irish poet, Sedulius, in
his "Easter Hymn" writes:

> Hail holy mother, who brought forth the king
> Who rules the heavens and the earth.
> He is God who rules forever, who encloses all
> in his power.
> Your blessed womb had the joys of motherhood with
> the honour of virginity.
> You alone of all women pleased Christ the Lord.
> There was none like you before you.
> There will be none like you after you.

Prayer to our Lady in the Church goes back to
well before the Council of Ephesus (431), as the
ancient prayer "We fly to thy patronage" *(Sub
tuum praesidium)* shows. By the time of Ephesus,
devotion to her was firmly rooted and formed a
significant element in people's faith. Cyril of
Alexandria wrote a wonderful and moving descript-
ion of the deposition of Nestorius who had
challenged Mary's right to be called "Mother of
God":

> Know then, that on the 22nd of June the Holy Synod
> met at Ephesus in the great Church . . . of Mary, the
> Mother of God. We spent the whole day there and
> finally . . . we deposed . . . Nestorius and removed him
> from the episcopal office. Now there were about 200
> or so of us bishops gathered together. And the whole

population of Ephesus was waiting tensely, waiting
from dawn to dusk for the decision of the Holy Synod.
When they heard that the unfortunate man had been
deposed, with one voice all started to shout in praise
of the Holy Synod, with one voice all began to glorify
God because the enemy of the faith had fallen.
When we left the church they escorted us to our
lodgings with torches; for it was evening. Gladness
was in the air; lamps dotted the city; even women
went before us with censers and led the way.

After Ephesus the position of the Mother of
God (Theotokos) was clear in the Christian faith.
An outstanding example of the way eastern
Christians combined solid doctrine and strong
personal affection for the Mother of God is
found in the "Akathistos Hymn" which dates
from the sixth century and which is one of the
most inspiring reflections on Mary ever written.

Devotion to our Lady is earlier in the eastern
Church than in the western but when the
western Church develops, it produces its own
particular and characteristic devotion to the
Mother of God. A fine example of this devotional
development are the hymns, often associated with
the Divine Office, which appear in the western
Church in the year 800 and following. These
hymns, like the "Ave Maris Stella" show a tender
and sincere devotion to Mary which is based on a
true understanding of her place in the plan of
salvation. These hymns place a greater emphasis
on the human Mary than do the hymns of the
East. This human note is evident also in the Irish
material of the period. The poems of Blathmac,
in particular, show that Mary was honoured,

revered, and loved in a truly sincere way by the ancient Irish.

Our Lady

The medieval Church is inconceivable without the Blessed Virgin Mary. She is the Woman, the ideal of womanhood, the Mother of the Saviour, Notre Dame, Our Lady. From among the many authors who wrote about her, Anselm, Bernard and Dante give us some idea of the strength and beauty of medieval devotion, as well as the great sense of closeness to her which Christians of that age had.

Decline

The names of Anselm, Bernard and Dante show that in the eleventh, twelfth and thirteenth centuries devotion to Mary was profound and balanced. This regrettably cannot be said of the two following centuries. The period before the Reformation shows a steady decline both in the balance and depth of devotion, and in the understanding of Mary's place in the plan of redemption. To anyone familiar with some of the puerile and superficial writing on devotion to Mary which marks this period, it is not a matter of wonder that the Protestant Reformation, when it came, produced a strong and hostile reaction to Marian piety in the forms it had assumed in the western Church.

Reform or over-correction

One of the lesser tragedies of the Reformation was the fact that in trying to correct abuses in devotion to our Lady, which were undoubtedly there in late medieval Catholic piety, the Reformers ended by misrepresenting, ignoring, even denying to Mary and to the saints their rightful place in the work of Christ. For this over-reaction, Catholic polemical writers were in part responsible. However, it is more to the point for us to realise that in the Reformation period two groups, each with a genuine devotion to Mary, clashed, and in the battle which ensued both were the losers, and the figure of the gentle Virgin of Nazareth was obscured by the stormy controversy. From the sixteenth-century Reformation to the present day there has been a gradual growing apart of Christians on the subject of Mary.

The earliest Protestant reformers, Martin Luther and Huldrich Zwingli, initially rejected very decisively some undoubted abuses and false ideas in the Marian devotional forms of the early sixteenth century. They quickly, however, came to reject the whole cult of the saints, including Mary. Catholic controversialists reacted strongly and tended to play down the abuses, just as the Lutheran, Zwinglian and (slightly later) the Calvinist polemic tended to play them up. The Reformation first set out to curb excesses in Marian devotion, but within a decade of Luther's first great commentaries, it had produced its own new and recognisably Protestant under-

standing of the Mother of God and her relation
to the salvation of men.

Even as Christians of the Reformation traditions played down Mary because they felt she had
been given a much too prominent place in late
medieval piety, so Catholics concentrated on her
more and more. Mariology, or the study and
defence of the privileges of Mary, emerged fully
as an inner Catholic discipline and increasingly, as
a special branch of theology with special rules. It
gradually asserts itself as the "Catholic" section
of theology in the minds of some, and Mary
comes to be seen more and more in much popular
piety as the typical Catholic devotional figure.
Devotion to her comes to be emphasised as the
hallmark of the devout Catholic.

In an age of fear

In the seventeenth and eighteenth centuries
the Catholic Church was deeply troubled by
Jansenism with its extremely rigorous doctrines
about human salvation. One of the counters to
this inhuman system was traditional Catholic devotion to the Mother of God. Many hard things
have been said about the Marian piety of St Louis
Marie de Montfort and St Alphonsus Liguori. It
should not be forgotten that the tremendous
influence which these saints give to the merciful
intercession of Mary is an attempt to bring hope
and joy into the lives of people living in an atmos-
phere poisoned by the impossible gospel of

Jansenism. In an age of fear, mercy is what they preach. But it is left to succeeding generations to realise the meaning of de Montfort's prophetic words about an "Age of Mary".

An "Age of Mary"?

The dialogue of popular piety, theological effort and official encouragement which character-ises the Marian movement of the nineteenth and the first half of the twentieth century began in 1831 with the revelation to St Catherine Labouré of the Miraculous Medal, a devotion soon approved and widely popular among the faithful.

1854 saw the definition of the Immaculate Conception, when, for the first time, a pope pronounced finally on a doctrine which was not in dispute in the Church, thus engaging the power of his teaching office and giving the Church its first Marian definition in more than 1,200 years. The century also saw Marian apparitions at La Salette (1846); Lourdes (1858); Pontmain, France, (1870); and at Knock, Ireland, in 1879.

In the eighteen eighties came the publication of the epoch-making Mariology of M.J. Scheeben of Cologne — a book which set new standards, and in its emphasis on Mary's inner relation to the Church took up a theme long lost sight of. Leo XIII, Pope from 1879-1901, gave a great impetus to the Marian movement by his encyclicals which emphasised Mary's intercessory power. In these he constantly, year after year,

hammered home the value of prayer to Mary,
particularly the rosary. It was during the pontificate of Leo XIII that the Marian congress, later
to become such a typical feature of the movement,
made its first appearance.

Pius X's most significant Marian statement was
his encyclical *Ad diem illum* on the fiftieth
anniversary of the Immaculate Conception definition. Benedict XV did not issue a special Marian
encyclical, but his statements on Mary's role in
redemption cannot be called reserved. 1917 saw
the foundation by Fr Maximilian Kolbe of the
Militia of the Immaculate Conception, the first
of the modern Marian mass-movements with
2,000,000 members. This same year saw the
apparition at Fatima. Parallel to the ever-growing
movement of Marian piety, came the further
apparitions of Beauraing (1932) and Banneaux
(1933) while the older shrines such as Lourdes
continued year by year to draw their pilgrims.

Even when the popes from Pius IX to XI did
not directly speak on Marian doctrine they often
gave an impetus to the Marian movement in other
ways. But in comparison with Pius XII these
pontifical interventions seem small and insignifi-
cant. They were nonetheless preparing the ground
for that astonishing upsurge of devotional
practice and doctrinal effort which were such a
marked feature of his pontificate. With Pius XII
the enthusiastic Mariologist's dream of an "Age
of Mary" seemed to have become a reality. In
1942 Pius XII consecrated the world to the
Immaculate Heart of Mary. In the next year,

1943, he produced the theologically compact
and complete Marian appendix to his encyclical
on the Church of that year. This pope expressed
himself again and again on the theme of Mary.
And to this constant encouragement popular
devotion and theological effort responded. The
Blessed Virgin gained more and more prominence
in the minds of the faithful.

The Second Vatican Council

The Second Vatican Council issued a very
important statement on Mary which emphasised
Mary's dependence on Christ and also that she
was model of the Church. In the conciliar statement there is no doubt that Christ is the "One
Mediator of God and man". Mary is very definitely
a secondary figure. But she has nonetheless a real
part in the salvation of man. The Vatican II
document is a fine summary of the best elements
in the Marian tradition of the Roman Catholic
Church. It avoids exaggerations about Mary; it
avoids evasions.
Paul VI's most significant document on Mary
was a needed corrective to certain attitudes which
had emerged in the Church after Vatican II. It is
a positive statement of the basic and inevitable
place Mary occupies in the scheme of salvation
and the need for us to recognise this in our
veneration. The Church expresses her faith most
definitely in her liturgy. In the liturgy Mary's
role in salvation appears clearly. She is also the

model of faith, and traditional devotional forms
like the Angelus and the Rosary are to be encouraged
because they bring this out. Mary is one who
receives the greatest grace and makes the most
perfect response to the Word of God.

1 FROM EAST AND WEST

From the East

Hail, by whom gladness will be enkindled;
hail, by whom the curse will be quenched.
Hail, righting of the fallen Adam;
hail, ransom of Eve's tears.
Hail, height unscaled by human reasonings;
hail, depth inscrutable even to angel's eyes.
Hail, for thou art the king's seat;
hail, for thou bearest him who bears all.
Hail, thou star that makest the sun to shine;
hail, thou womb of God's Incarnation.
Hail, thou by whom all creation is renewed;
hail, thou through whom the Creator became a babe.
Hail, Mother undefiled.

This beautiful hymn to Mary (the Akathistos
hymn) is still sung in the eastern liturgy. It is
at least 1,300 years old and possibly considerably
older. The stanza quoted above is the first of a
series of acclamations or praises of Mary, composed
for the feast of the Annunciation. This feast was
celebrated in the eastern Church even before the
Council of Ephesus, and was seen as a celebration
of the Incarnation, God coming among us as a

man. This was a feast of great joy as it marked
the beginning of our redemption. The Akathistos
hymn is a hymn to the mystery of the Incarnation.
It underlines the kindliness, wisdom and power
of God which are evident to the faithful in this
mystery but hidden from the worldly-wise. Mary
appears as one who is brought into the inscrutable
plans of God, to be the Virgin Mother of his Son.
She is not seen alone but as called to have part
in the mystery of Christ.

The Akathistos hymn is sung solemnly in its
entirety on the fifth Saturday in Lent. It is called
Akathistos (which means not-sitting) from the
fact that, to emphasise the dignity of the mystery
it celebrates, the ritual forbids participants to
be seated. The hymn, which is very long, contains
320 verses. It is made up of twelve narrative
stanzas, twelve lyrical stanzas, twelve hymns of
praise each made up of twelve invocations,
twelve repetitions of the Marian refrain: "Hail,
Mother Undefiled", and twelve Alleluias. A
reading of the entire hymn bears out that it is
"the most beautiful, the most profound and the
most ancient Marian hymn in all Christian literature".

The twelve narrative stanzas tell in verse of
incidents in the infancy of Christ taken from St
Luke's Gospel. They are followed by a reflective
lyrical verse which meditates on the biblical
mystery. Each reflective stanza in turn is
followed by twelve invocations or acclamations
to Mary. These are based on the mystery which
has just been narrated and reflected on. Thus the
baffling of human wisdom by the great mystery

of the Incarnation causes the poet to write these
meditative words:

> The garrulous rhetors
>   became as dumb as fishes
>   before thee, O Mother of God.
> We see them toiling in vain to say
>   how, remaining a virgin, thou couldst
>   beget.
> But we, marvelling at the mystery,
>   cry out in faith.
> Hail! receptacle
>   of God's wisdom.
> Hail, treasury
>   of his providence.
> Hail, thou who showest
>   the ignorance of philosophers.
> Hail, thou who makest speechless
>   the men of science.
> Hail, for the makers of myths
>   stopped their stories.

Titles of rare beauty abound in this wonderful
Marian hymn as the poet, struck by the angel's
words, *Hail, full of grace,* weaves pattern after
pattern of praise on this same theme.

> Hail, flashing example of resurrection.
> Hail, beginning of all Christ's wonders.
> Hail, summary of all teachings about him.
> Hail, Mother undefiled.

From the West

> Hail, Star of the Sea,
> Tender Mother of God,
> Ever Virgin,
> Blessed Gate of Heaven.

These are the opening words of an old and beautiful hymn to Mary that we know in Latin as "Ave Maris Stella". It was written between 600 and 800 A.D. and is found in a manuscript of the ninth century which is now in the Abbey of St Gallen (called after the Irish monk St Gall), in Switzerland. The author is no longer known, but a reading of the hymn shows he had a tender devotion to the Mother of God and a simple and direct piety. The hymn recalls the greeting of the angel (in Latin *Ave*) and points to Mary as the one in whom not merely the role but even the very name of Eve is reversed (*Eva/Ave*). Mary is called on to ask for all good things for us — that we may be freed from our sins, get light in our blindness, and that evil may be driven from us.

> Show thyself a mother.
> May he who was born for us as your Son
> Receive our prayers through you.

Mary is the Mother of Christ, our Saviour; she is also, the next stanza reminds us, a model for us to imitate. If we are meek like her we are following her Son who said: "Learn of me, for I am meek and humble of heart." The motherly role of Mary in our Christian lives is to lead us to Jesus. To see Jesus in his glory is our destiny, the joy which cannot fail. It is to him Mary brings us. The hymn closes with words of praise of God, Father, Son, and Holy Spirit.

The hymn "Ave Maris Stella" brings clearly before us the story of the salvation of men as the gospels describe it. Mary, the Virgin, is the gate through which the King of Heaven enters the

world. In her free decision to say "Yes" to God
she becomes Mother of God and associated in
the work of her Son. She has a motherly care
for all of us. We are his brothers and sisters. She
assists us as we make our way towards God. Her
concern is that we come to Jesus at the end and
that all honour and glory of our saving be given
to God who saves us.

The hymn is set to a simple melody which
enhances the delicate feeling for and the keen
devotional sense of Mary's part in our salvation
which the words express so finely.

Two great Marian antiphons

The sense the Church has always had of the
abiding and protective presence of Mary, God's
gift to us, is perhaps nowhere more beautifully
expressed than in the age-old custom of conclud-
ing the divine office with a hymn to our Blessed
Lady. Among hymns used in this way are the
"Hail, Holy Queen" ("Salve Regina"), and "Tender
Mother of the Redeemer" ("Alma Redemptoris
Mater"). These two hymns to our Lady are only
a tiny sample of the many lovely Marian hymns
which have come down to us from the past. Like
so many other hymns to Mary these two express
simply and lovingly man's astonishment and
wonder at the greatness of what God has done for
her. They express, too, a confidence in her
motherly help, and make a frank and clear
admission of man's weakness and of his sinfulness before God.

To the astonishment of nature you have borne the
One who gave you life . . . Come to the aid of your
people who are always falling, but keep struggling to
arise.

The "Hail, Holy Queen" is again the prayer
the sinner makes to Mary, the Mother of Mercy.
Indeed it is more accurately the prayer *we sinners*
make to Mary, our Mother. The hymn emphasises
our pilgrim status, our exile from the Lord *(cf.
2 Cor 5:6)*, and our need of Mary's motherly
help in our sinfulness. Her part is to lead us to
Jesus in glory. She is the Mother of Mercy. But
Jesus is Mercy itself, God's mercy made flesh,
our only Saviour.

There is an old Gaelic poem written about the
year 700 which is headed: "It is Blathmac, son
of Cu Brettan, son of Congus of the Fir Rois
has made this devoted offering to Mary and her
Son." It is a lament for the dead Christ. Recently
the poems of Blathmac, together with the Irish
gospel of Thomas and a poem on the Virgin
Mary, were edited with a translation by Professor
James Carney of the Dublin Institute of Advanced
Studies. The poems and the Irish gospel of
Thomas had been discovered by Professor Carney
in the National Library of Ireland.

By far the most important part of the material
published by Professor Carney consists of the
lengthy poem or poems ascribed to Blathmac,
son of Cu Brettan. The first poem consists of
149 stanzas. It is probable that a single stanza
has been accidentally dropped and that the full
poem had the mystic 150, a quatrain for every
psalm in the Psalter. The second poem refers
to the first and is, in fact, a continuation of it.
Only 109 quatrains can be read in full due to
staining and loss of leaves. It is possible that this
second poem may originally have consisted of

150 stanzas also. The two poems which the manuscript contains are related in theme. Each of
them is addressed to Mary and focuses on Christ
her Son and on the great and glorious adventure
of his life, death and resurrection. These are
recalled to Mary in great detail. In the first poem
lamentation with Mary for the sufferings and
death of her Son is the dominant theme. In the
second, Christ's victory, the judgment by the
Victorious Son and his avenging of the blood of
the innocent are stressed.

First poem

The poet has an obviously deep and personal
sense of relationship to Mary. He is writing a
lament or keen (caoineadh), but it is a lament
with Mary for the sufferings of her Son. The
poet is not insensitive to Mary's sufferings, but
it is the tribulations of Christ, whom he sees as
the great captive, which grip him. The poem
opens:

> Come to me, loving Mary, that I may keen with you
> your very dear one. Alas that your Son should go to the
> cross, he who was a great diadem, a beautiful hero.

> That with you I may beat my two hands for the
> captivity of your beautiful Son: your womb has
> conceived Jesus — it has not marred your virginity.

The quality of lament comes through particularly
in the closing verses of the poem where the poet
wishes for power over the people of the world "as
far as every sea" so that they would come and
keen the royal Son of Mary.

After the opening verses which set the tone of
the poem as a lament, the poet passes to praise of
Jesus as a child, and mentions the notable events
which marked his childhood, dwelling, in particular,
on the Matthean Magi story. He then turns to the
goodness of Jesus as shown in his public ministry.
His treatment of this could be described as a
meditative commentary on the passage in Acts
which shows "how God anointed Jesus of
Nazareth with the Holy Spirit and with power;
how he went about doing good and healing all
that were oppressed by the devil, for God was with
him" *(Acts 10:38).* The poet contrasts sharply
the goodness and kindness of Jesus towards men
with the ingratitude men showed towards him
in putting him to death unjustly. Then he outlines
for Mary the good deeds of her Son for men:

> Bestowal of food on every pauper, raiment from him
> to every naked one; for the Son of the living God had
> taught that everyone would be the better for mercy.

> It is certain that these were the deeds of your great
> beautiful Son, Mary: the ceaseless endowing of each
> one, bounty and generosity.

> It is manifest then that he was the Son of God whose
> attributes were the blameless cure of bodies and the
> full cure of souls.

Beautiful Mary

The poet's attitude towards Mary is one of
tremendous confidence. There is a gentle and
personal note in his addresses. Mary is very

definitely one of us. Her humanness is very clear.
She is not some remote celestial being but the
earthly mother of the Lord. This is most clear
in those passages where the poet directly
addresses her. These have been described as
exhibiting "not merely tenderness but startling
intimacy". There is a directness and spontaneity
in them which shows the existence of a tradition
of confident piety and devotion to her. The
certainty which is expressed here is something
which matures slowly. The people from whom
this poem comes had given "the Mother of the
great Lord" a place in their stories and in their
hearts.

Christ, the Victor, is Mary's Son

The poems constantly affirm the close association that exists between Christ and his mother.
Yet there is no doubt that it is Christ who alone
vanquishes his enemies. It is Mary's Son who is
the conquering hero. And he is this precisely
because he is at one and the same time God's
Son, the Son of the Father to whom he is perfectly
obedient. The poet observes that it is from Mary's
Son that true filial piety is learnt. He was obedient
to death.

Second poem

After this account of the earthly life and
glorification of Jesus, the second poem goes on

to emphasise the divinity of the Son of Mary
and his power. Some verses are devoted to the
Eucharist, the body and blood of Mary's Son, our
Saviour. The theme of Jesus risen from the dead,
ascended and sending the Spirit , is taken up and
developed, and his power is underlined.
Prophecies foretelling him are dealt with and
lastly the poem offers a treatment of the Judgment as judgment by Jesus, as the vindication of
the just and their revenge for their torments.

Christ is the one who, apparently vanquished
and put down by his many enemies, is buried
without the princely lament which is his due.
But Mary's Son was the victor in the great battle
with evil. He crushed the devil and bound him.
Christ, Mary's Son, is the one who arises at
Easter in triumph and takes his seat in victory
at the right hand of his Father.

> He then returned to his body when he cast off the
> great attack and he arose (bright tidings!) on Easter
> day, after three days. His crucified body was his
> victory . . .
> Happy for your Son, whom you have reared alone . . .
> He took over rule; he chose his kingly seat;
> he sat with victorious valour on the right-hand side
> of God, the Father.

And to Mary the poet says:

> This is what this signifies: the Son you have borne,
> Mary, will be Lord without beginning, and Lord
> without any end.

3 THEY CALLED HER "OUR LADY"

Anselm

Mary, great Mary,
most blessed of all Marys,
greatest among all women,
great Lady, great beyond measure,
I long to love you with all my heart;
I want to praise you with my lips;
I desire to venerate you in my understanding;
I love to pray to you from my deepest being,
I commit myself wholly to your protection.

The scholar Anselm was born in 1033 in Aosta, then in the kingdom of Burgundy. He entered the abbey of Notre Dame at Bec in Normandy and became prior at the age of thirty. During his time at Bec he wrote three beautiful prayers to our Lady. He sent these to his well-loved friend, the monk Gundolf, with the address:

There is no need for me to say much about how long our friendship has lasted, to one who I know is my other self in the bond of love. Let me say this briefly about us — my love for you has never diminished by any change in me from its first beginning and I am careful that alteration shall always serve only to increase it.

And of the prayers themselves he writes:

> So accept them for they have been made with you
> in mind, and do not blame me for their length,
> which was made at the request of someone else. And
> would that they might be so long that before whoever
> was reading them — or better still meditating on them,
> since that is what they are meant for — came to the
> end, he might be pierced by contrition or by love,
> through which we reach a concern for heavenly things.

The three prayers form a certain unity. The first prayer is a prayer to be offered to our Lady when the mind is weighed down with heaviness. The second passes a stage beyond this and is to be said when the mind is anxious with fear. This is the prayer of the sinner who has been raised from the torpor brought on by many sins and is now looking towards God for forgiveness but is rightly anxious with fear because of his sins. The third prayer puts the emphasis on the purifying of the sinner's love, and particularly asks Mary for her own and for Christ's love. The prayers thus represent three stages of the soul's movement from sin towards God. Mary appears in a slightly different role in each prayer but always as the helper of the sinner. Mary, the holy one, presents such a contrast to the wretched condition of the sinner that he is confused. Nonetheless he still calls for help:

> The brightness of your holiness confounds the dark-
> ness of my sins but surely you will not blush to feel
> kindness to such a wretch? . . .
> Lady, before God and before you my sins appear vile
> and therefore so much the more do they need his
> healing and your help.

A mind anxious with fear

The sinner, made aware of his sins, is afraid.
In his beautiful second prayer Anselm shows him
that if he fears, rightly because he is a sinner, he
hopes rightly because he has found a Saviour,
"the Son of Man, who came to seek that which
was lost". Mary is seen to be caught up and
involved deeply in the mercifulness of this Son of
Man.

> The Son of Man in his goodness came of his own free
> will to save that which was lost;
> how can the Mother of God not care when the lost
> cry to her?
> The Son of Man came to "call sinners to repentance"—
> how can the Mother of God despise the prayers of the
> repentant?
> The good God, the gentle man, the merciful Son of God,
> the good Son of Man, came to seek the sinner who
> had strayed; and will you, good mother of the man,
> mighty Mother of God, repel wretches who pray to you?

There is a tremendous stress on the common
bond of humanity that unites God become man,
the sinner who calls for his mercy and the Virgin
Mother of the Son. The bond which binds the
Son and the Mother involves them both in the
sinner's plight. Anselm writes of himself: "Indeed
I am the sinner who belongs to you both." The
Son is human son and the Mother is human
mother "for the salvation of sinners".

> O human virgin, of you was born a human God,
> to save human sinners; and see, before both Son and
> mother, is a human sinner, penitent and confessing,
> groaning and praying . . .

The Son and the Mother

There is a striking insistence in the prayer on
the bond of Son and Mother. They are together.
If the sinner turns from the Son he turns from
the Mother. If he makes the Mother his refuge, he
is calling on the mercy of the Son.

In a magnificent appeal to both Anselm prays:

> God, who was made the Son of a woman out of mercy;
> woman who was made Mother of God out of mercy;
> have mercy upon this wretch,
> You (i.e. Christ) forgiving, you (i.e. Mary) interceding,
> or show the unhappy man to whom he may flee for safety
> and point out in whose power he may more certainly
> confide.

It belongs to your Son

Anselm's unbounded confidence in Mary and
the strength of his prayer to her is not some
aberration but an expression of his need for the
Saviour Christ, the Son of God. He has
great reverence for Christ's human mother, who
is "above all" but "after the Lord, who is my
God, my all, your Son".

To Christ, Anselm speaks at the end of his
third prayer:

> Lover and ruler of mankind,
> you could love those who accused you even to death
> and can you refuse when you are asked
> those who love you and your Mother?

And to Mary:

> Mother of our Lover, who carried him in her womb
> and was willing to give him milk at her breast —
> are you not able or are you unwilling to grant your
> love to those who ask it?
> Oh rich in saving grace, your Son is the reconciliation
> of sinners.
> For there is no reconciliation except that which you
> conceived in chastity,
> there is no salvation except that which you brought
> forth as virgin.
> Therefore, Lady,
> you are mother of justifier and the justified,
> bearer of reconciliation and the reconciled,
> parent of Salvation and of the saved.

Bernard

Bernard of Clairvaux (1153) is a name associated
for generations past with devotion to our Lady.
That he was greatly devoted to her is beyond
question. He was described as a pupil of hers. . .
alumnus enim familiarissimus Dominae nostrae,
(PL202, 618A). But he was by no means uncritical,
as his famous letter to the Canons of the Church
of Lyons shows. In this letter he, in spite of his
great devotion to Mary, shows himself to be
opposed to the newly-introduced feast of the
Immaculate Conception, basically because he
felt it as a novelty. Bernard was a very conservative
man at heart. But in this instance his conservatism
led him astray. He opposed what was, in fact, the
work of the Holy Spirit, as later generations of
Christians recognised.

Bernard's praise of Mary is sincere, profound and poetic but extremely traditional. What he emphasises about her is what he has received from the past. He does not introduce new things. "What he has received from the Church", that is what he values and proclaims:

> You say that the Mother of the Lord should be highly honoured. You are right, but "the honour of the queen loves justice". The Virgin has many true titles to honour, many real marks of dignity, and does not need any that are false. Let us honour her for the purity of her body, the holiness of her life. Let us marvel at her fruitful virginity, and venerate her divine Son. Let us extol her freedom from concupiscence in conceiving, and from all pain in bearing. Let us proclaim her to be reverenced by the angels, desired by the nations, foretold by the patriarchs and prophets, chosen out of all and preferred before all. Let us magnify her as the channel of grace, the mediatrix of salvation, the restorer of the ages, and as exalted above the choirs of angels to the very heights of heaven. All this the Church sings in her praise and teaches me too to sing. What I have received from the Church I firmly cling to and confidently pass on to others; but, I confess, I am chary of admitting anything that I have not received from her.

There is a certain magnificence about Bernard's confidence in Mary which is expressed so well in what is perhaps the best-known passage in all that he wrote — the "Star of the Sea" passage in one of his commentaries. In this beautiful and poetic passage the leitmotiv is the name of Mary, invoked again and again:

> In danger, in all need, in doubt think of Mary, call on Mary. Let her name be ever on your lips and never absent from you heart.

In Bernard, as in Anselm, there speaks the
humility of medieval man. Man, big enough to
acknowledge his weakness and his need of God to
bind up his sinfulness through the power of Christ
and the ministering gentleness of his Mother.

> May he be silent about your mercy, Blessed Virgin,
> if there should exist one who has called on you in
> his necessities and remembers that you have failed him.

Dante

In the thirty-third Canto of the Paradiso,
Divina Commedia, it is Bernard who prays the
magnificent prayer to the Virgin Mary with
which the canto opens. In this prayer again we
find that marvellous understanding of the ways
of God with man which characterises the Marian
tradition. The inevitability of Mary for the
sinner — the need to acknowledge God's tender
purposes — these are the themes which show
that the poet is a man of the medieval world.

> Lady so great and powerful
> — he who seeks grace apart from thee
> flies without wings.
>
> Your tenderness is help. Even before
> we ask, you run to our assistance.
>
> Compassion, pity, all the magnificence
> of man — these are in you — are yours.

Luther: Empty hands before God

The "great things" are nothing less than that she
became the mother of God, in which work so many
and such great good things are bestowed on her as
pass man's understanding. For on this there follows
all honour, all blessedness, and her unique place in
the whole of mankind, among which she has no equal,
namely, that she had a child by the Father in heaven,
and such a Child. She herself is unable to find a name
for this work, it is too exceedingly great; all she can
do is break out in the fervent cry: "they are great
things", impossible to describe or define. Hence, men
have crowded all her glory into a single word, calling
her the Mother of God. No one can say anything
greater of her or to her, though he had as many tongues
as there are leaves on the trees or grass in the fields or
stars in the sky or sand by the sea. It needs to be
pondered in the heart what it means to be the Mother
of God.

These inspiring words on Mary were written by
Martin Luther in the opening months of the year
1521 in his *Commentary on the Magnificat*. This
Commentary, though a small book, is one which
contains many fine things about Mary. It expresses
with great force a very keen sense of Mary's little-

ness, her nothingness before God. It is a book
which conveys a tremendous sense of God as God.

The simplicity of Mary

Luther's portrait of Mary in the Commentary
places great emphasis on her lowliness and simplicity. She is a peasant girl from Nazareth. She is the
truly humble person who does not know her own
humility. She is content to spend her days not
looking to be honoured or exalted, or even becoming
aware of her humility. She is poor and despised.
The coming of God's messenger to her to tell her
the astonishing news of her vocation does not change
her. She remains the same as she was — humble,
accepting God's grace in simplicity of heart and
giving God the glory. Luther writes:

> She is not puffed up, does not vaunt herself or proclaim
> with a loud voice that she is to become the Mother of
> God. She seeks not any glory but goes about her usual
> household duties, milking the cows, cooking the meals,
> washing pots and kettles, sweeping out the rooms and
> performing the work of maidservant or housewife in
> lowly and despised tasks, as though she cared nothing
> for such great gifts and graces . . . Oh how simple and
> pure a heart was hers! How marvellous a human being
> is here! What great things are hidden here under this
> lowly exterior.

He who is mighty

Luther presents Mary as one of us, as someone
who lived out her life on earth in circumstances

like ours. This starting point allows him to place a strong emphasis on the fact that she depends absolutely on God's grace. The fact that she calls herself a simple servant-maid underlines her closeness to us and her sense of how far removed from the greatness and holiness of God she is. She is the humble servant-maid who can acknowledge fully that all she has is from the Lord. She consciously stands before God with empty hands and is filled with good things out of his boundless kindness. We can recognise her as one of us and see the greatness of the gifts she received. We can learn to believe in God's generous intent towards us:

> O Blessed Virgin, Mother of God, what great comfort God has shown us in you, by so graciously regarding your unworthiness and low estate. This encourages us to believe that henceforth he will not despise us poor and lowly ones but graciously regard us also, according to your example.

But it is God who is the Giver. He is the source of all good gifts. It is he, the One who is mighty, who has done "great things" for Mary and who will do great things for us.

The tender Mother of God

At the beginning and end of Luther's Magnificat Commentary we find two beautiful prayers to our Lady:

> May the tender Mother of God herself procure for me the spirit of wisdom, profitably and thoroughly to

expound this song of hers, so that Your Grace as well
as we all may draw from it wholesome knowledge and
a praiseworthy life and thus come to chant and sing
this Magnificat eternally in heaven. To this may God
help us. Amen.

We pray God to give us a right understanding of this
Magnificat, an understanding that consists not merely
in brilliant words but in glowing life in body and soul.
May Christ grant us this through the intercession
and for the sake of his dear Mother Mary.

God is the Almighty, the All-Holy

God is the source of all gifts. Christ is the great
gift in whom all other gifts are given. It is necessary
to have a clear grasp of this to properly appreciate
the role of the "tender Mother of God".

Luther is clearly concerned that there are people
who do not see, even with the clear example of
the life and words of Mary, the Mother of God,
before their eyes, that man cannot have merit
against God. He asserts in the face of all attempts
to put some human reality — be it works or merit
or saint or even Mother of God — in place of God,
that this is idolatry. God alone is God. To his
name alone must praise be given. The Magnificat
makes clear how well Mary understands this
absolutely fundamental truth of the Christian
faith that God is the All-Mighty, the All-Holy.

Luther is trying all through his Commentary
on the Magnificat to bring Mary down to the level
of ordinary people. He wants them to see her

primarily as a recipient of God's grace. They
have tended to contrast themselves with her as
with someone raised far above them. Luther wants
to restore the proportions. He is interested before
all else in emphasising to his contemporaries the
abyss between Mary, the creature, and God, her
creator. He thus dwells on her ordinariness as the
maiden from Nazareth rather than on her greatness as "Queen of Heaven". He insists on her grace
as Theotokos as something totally undeserved.
And he reserves his severest words for those who
seem to regard her as a helper independent of God.

Luther, with many in his age, had inherited a
highly distorted understanding of the place of Mary
and the saints in the life of the Christian. He, with
others, made significant efforts to remove this
distortion. Ultimately he jettisoned a good deal
of the Marian understanding and piety in which he
had grown up. But his earlier efforts were not to
get rid of this traditional Catholic propensity but
to purify and renew it. The Magnificat Commentary
represents the high-water-mark of these efforts.

Erasmus: Will you turn my Son out, too?

> How many there are who put more trust in the safe-
> guard of the Virgin Mary or St Christopher than of
> Christ himself. They worship the Mother with images,
> candles and songs, and offend Christ grievously by
> their evil living.

The quotation is taken from the writings of
Desiderius Erasmus, Dutch humanist, brilliant
scholar, near-contemporary of Martin Luther.

Like Luther and many others of the time, Erasmus
was disturbed at the poor, even corrupt, state of
popular devotion to the saints and the Blessed
Virgin. He feels that some people mistakenly pray
to the Blessed Virgin as more trustworthy than
Christ — a foolish, even blasphemous, error. They
compound the error by having a devotion to Mary
which is purely external and false, for their lives
are evil and offend Christ, our Lord. It was such
hypocrisy in popular devotion to Mary and the
saints that led Erasmus and others to attack this
devotion vehemently and to call for its reform.
Not all voices, however, were as moderate as
Erasmus and the calls for reform were soon
succeeded, particularly among the Protestant
Reformers, by calls for total abolition. Erasmus
then found himself caught between an exaggerated
and near-superstitious Catholic devotion to Mary
and Protestant voices calling for a total abolition
of Marian devotion altogether. He was well aware
of the need for a very severe purging of much
that had grown up around devotion to our Lady
in the Catholic Church in the Middle Ages:

> A mariner in a storm is more ready to invoke the
> Mother of Christ or St Christopher or some one or
> other of the saints than Christ himself. And they
> think they have made the Virgin their friend by
> singing her in the evening the little song, *Salve Regina;*
> they have more reason to be afraid that the Virgin
> should think that they jeer her by their singing for
> their whole day and a great part of the night is spent
> in obscene talk and drunkenness and things which
> are not fit to be mentioned.

Erasmus, however, was able to see clearly that
what had happened in the Church was due to the
fallibility and weakness of man. Something good
had gone sour. Devotion to Mary and the saints had
become distorted; it needed correction. To say
that it should be abolished was to take away
something from Christianity. It was like cutting
off one's head to cure a headache.

The position of Erasmus is put very clearly in
a dialogue of his called the *Religious Pilgrimage.*
Here he is severely critical of abuses but very
firm against any attempt to get rid of our Lady
and the saints altogether. His standpoint is put
beautifully in a mythical letter which he claims
our Blessed Lady wrote to a Lutheran called
Glaucoplutus.

The Letter to Glaucoplutus

In this letter the Blessed Virgin begins by pointing out that the Lutherans have done for her one
favour, in that their opposition to devotion to her
has at least prevented people from asking her for
things that are positively wicked.

> The wicked soldier who butchers men for money bawls
> out to me with these words, "O Blessed Virgin, send
> me rich plunder!" . . . The usuerer prays, "Help me to
> a large interest on my money!"

But the letter goes on to make clear that there
has been a dramatic falling off in true devotion to
our Lady:

Before this I was called Queen of the Heavens and Empress of the World, but now there are very few from whom I hear a "Hail Mary". Formerly I was adorned with gold and jewels and had many changes of apparel, I had presents made to me of gold and jewels but now I have scarce half a vest to cover me and that is mouse-eaten too. My yearly revenue is scarcely enough to keep alive my poor little clerk who lights for me a small wax or tallow candle.

The Reform has gone very far. But it means to go further. It means to "strip the altars and temples of the saints everywhere". Mary warns against this in a low-key ironic vein, pointing out that the saints will not stand for it. For Peter has the Keys of the Kingdom. Paul has a sword. And George is all in armour. They will not be so easily turned out. Then, at the very end of the letter comes the point: Mary is unlike Peter or Paul or George on horseback, the knight in shining armour. She has no weapons. She is the Mother and she has only her Son:

> You shall not turn me out, unless you turn my Son out too, whom I hold in my arms. I won't be pulled away from him. *You shall either throw us both out or leave us both unless you have a mind to have a Church without a Christ.*

The solidity, balance and true fervour of the devotion to Mary of Erasmus is not in doubt. A prayer of his shows this clearly:

> O Mary, who alone of all women are mother and virgin, the happiest of mothers and the purest of virgins, we who are impure come to visit and address ourselves to you who are pure and to reverence you with our poor offerings, such as they are. May your Son enable us to imitate your most holy life, that we may deserve by

the grace of the Holy Spirit, to conceive the Lord Jesus
in our hearts and never to lose him. Amen.

Erasmus's genuine piety towards Mary and his
intuitive grasp of the God-given place of Mary in
the work of Christ did not blind him to the abuses
in devotion to Mary and the saints which were
rightly stigmatised by the Reformers. He himself
was a severe critic of these abuses. But he stood
for renewal of a true understanding and a true
devotional life based on the communion of saints.
He saw that to lessen the role of Christ's members
in one another's salvation was ultimately to
depreciate the work of Christ and God the Spirit,
whose "living temples" they were. No Christ
without Mary. No Church without Christ.

Calvin: The honour which is hers

As far as we are concerned we wish to regard her as she
wishes to be regarded, namely as the Holy Ghost teaches
us to regard her. But we must not just praise her in
word, we must follow her example. The greatest praise
we can offer is when we recognise her as our teacher
and become her pupils . . . We . . . wish to follow her
example and realising that God in his grace has looked
on her, we wish to see in her, as in a mirror, the mercy
of God. He has saved us from the abyss. He has chosen
us for no other reason than that he is the source of every
good thing and our misery moves him to mercy and
compassion.

If we realise that the Virgin Mary has offered herself
to us as an example; if we confess with her that we are
nothing, that we are useless, and that all we have is from
the sheer goodness of God, then we are truly pupils of

Mary and show that we have grasped her teaching.
What greater honour could we show her than this?

These words were written in the middle of the
sixteenth century by John Calvin, one of the
founding fathers of the Protestant Reform. Calvin
was a very severe critic of what he considered
abuses in the Marian devotion of his time. He
was very concerned to place a strong emphasis on
the imitation of Mary. He did this partly because
he felt that there were far too many people who
were prepared to rely on Mary while making no
effort to live according to the demands of her
Son's gospel. He rightly saw this attitude as a
perversion of Christianity. He felt that he must
protest when the honour which belongs to God
alone was given to a creature — Mary. Such behaviour
dishonours Mary rather than honours her:

> We truly do not want to take in the least from the
> honour which is her (i.e. Mary's) due, but nothing is
> withheld from her by not making her into a goddess.
> On the contrary people do Mary a great disservice
> when they disfigure her with false praise and rob
> God of what belongs to him.

Learning from Mary

In Calvin's view there are very many things
we can learn from Mary. Her faith is exemplary.
So is her humility and her obedience. She is a
model for us in her knowledge of the Scripture
as shown in the Magnificat hymn. In particular
her words on God's mercy being "from generation to generation to those that fear him"

(Lk 1:50), echo the words of the Old Testament
book of Exodus where God proclaims that he
will show "steadfast love to thousands of those
who love me and keep my commandments"
(Exod 20:6).

Mary challenges us by her example to give
ourselves over into God's hands, to follow wherever
his word calls us, to offer whatever service he
demands of us. This is the truth of Mary's vocation
and life. She is to be praised precisely for this that
she accepted God's word sent to her through the
angel as a word to be obeyed in faith. Calvin writes:

> This is the principal virtue that we see in the Virgin
> Mary that she does not judge things by our human
> standards but according to the decision she made in
> the power of the Holy Spirit.

Mary, mother of men

John Calvin presents a strongly moralistic
portrait of Mary. He lays a necessary emphasis
on the littleness of Mary before God and on the
need for those who would praise her to imitate
her example. What a Catholic misses in John
Calvin, however, is the human warmth of his own
Catholic Marian tradition. The confident
spontaneity with which generation after generation of Christians took Mary for their mother
is missing here. And because this is so, a new
and more metallic Christianity emerges. The
heart is silent. The Gospel is no longer a fully
human gospel. The Mother of the Lord is no
longer the mother of men.

Anglicanism: that silent faithful figure

And as Anglicans, too, we must be grateful that
within our Church, the tradition of devotion to the
Blessed Mother has never altogether died away. For,
indeed, wherever the Magnificat is recited daily at
evensong, and the feasts of the Purification and the
Annunciation observed, and the Gospel records
read and meditated on in this context, there thank-
fulness and love towards that silent, faithful figure
can never wholly fail to spring forth. And that
quiet unobtrusive tradition of devotion might be
seen best summed up, in the words of a hymn
written in the early years of the nineteenth century
before the Oxford Movement gave a sudden new
impetus to the praise of Blessed Mary . . .

Virgin-born we bow before thee;
Blessed was the womb that bore thee
Mary, Mother meek and mild
Blessed was she in her Child.

Blessed was the breast that fed thee.
Blessed was the hand that led thee.
Blessed was the parent's eye
That watched thy slumbering infancy.

Blessed she by all creation
Who brought forth the world's salvation,
And blessed they — for ever blest
Who love thee most and serve thee best.

Virgin-born we bow before thee;
Blessed was the womb that bore thee.
Mary, Mother meek and mild
Blessed was she in her Child.

Anglicans to a greater degree than Calvinists
or continental Lutherans have preserved within
their Communion a tradition of devotion to the

Mother of God. This tradition has waxed and
waned but never altogether died. At the
Reformation there was a great break in the
Anglican Church with medieval devotional
practice. Walsingham in Norfolk, one of the
greatest shrines of medieval England, was
totally destroyed. Statues of our Lady disappeared and many holy places were closed. Almost
the whole liturgical veneration of Mary was
removed from the Prayer Book and Invocation
of Mary totally forbidden. This break in popular
devotion was partly a protest against certain
corrupt forms which popular religion had taken.
In spite of this we still find a hundred years
later evidence of the persistence of a spirit of
devotion to Mary within Anglicanism:

> How gladly do we second the angel in praise of her,
> which was more ours than his. How justly do we
> bless her, whom the angel pronounced blessed! How
> worthily is she honoured of men whom the angel
> proclaims beloved of God. O blessed Mary he cannot
> bless thee, he cannot honour thee too much, that
> deifies thee not. That which the angel said of thee
> thou has prophesied of thyself; we believe the
> angel and thee: All generations shall call thee blessed,
> by the fruit of whose womb all generations are
> blessed.
> **Bishop Hall** (1574-1656)

> In respect of her it was therefore necessary that we
> might perpetually preserve an esteem of her person
> proportionate to so high a dignity. It was her own
> prediction, "From henceforth all generations shall
> call me blessed"; but the obligation is ours to call
> her so, to esteem her so . . . We cannot bear too
> reverent a regard unto "the Mother of our Lord"

so long as we give her not that worship which is due
to the Lord himself.
Bishop Pearson (1612-1686)

In these two quotations we see the clear
affirmation of the "reverent regard" (Pearson),
and "honour" (Hall) due to Mary the Mother
of the Lord. At the same time we find a certain
fear of excess, a fear that people would forget
that Mary was only a creature and would say
too much of her. These marks characterise
Anglican devotion to Mary. Bishop Pearson also
expresses himself very clearly on Christ and
Mary:

Let us keep the language of the primitive Church:
Let her be honoured and esteemed: let Him be
worshipped and adored.

This last phrase is a quotation from St
Epiphanius (403 A.D.) and indicates the
importance Anglicans attach to the witness
of the early centuries.

The Oxford movement

In the nineteenth century we find a strong
upsurge of devotion to the Mother of God
within Anglicanism. This is due, partly at least,
to a renewed interest in the writings of the
Fathers of the Church. Even the controversies
about the Church between Newman, now a
Roman Catholic, and E.B. Pusey cannot obscure
the common bond of affection for the Mother
of God which binds them. Newman points out

to Pusey that the rigours of controversy and his
zeal in attacking what he sees as Roman
Catholic excesses about Mary may have had
effects beyond what he intended:

> Have you not been touching us on a very tender
> point in a very rude way? Is it not the effect of
> what you have said to expose her to scorn and
> obloquy, who is dearer to us than any other
> creature? Have you even hinted that our love for
> her is anything else than an abuse? Have you thrown
> her one kind word yourself all through your book?
> I trust so, but I have not lighted upon one. And yet
> I know you love her well.

But already in his "Eirenicon", the book which
Newman has just been criticising, Pusey himself
seems to have sensed the lack of a certain
spontaneity and fullness in Anglican Marian
devotion at this time:

> But negatively, I own that we have been in this
> respect in an unnatural state. Our hearts have been
> cramped. We have not, many of us, been able to
> give full scope to our feelings, nor have we ventured
> to dwell on the mysteries connected with the Mother
> of our Lord and God. I know not whether you found
> it so when among us, that even your tender heart dared
> not pour out its tenderness just in this special subject,
> where it would flow most naturally. I know not
> and do not wish to draw out anything from your
> heart's sanctuary. If it was not so you were, in this
> too, an exception.

Newman, already as an Anglican, was a stout
defender of Mary and came in his accession to the
Roman Church to realise clearly that "devotion to
Mary is integral to the worship of Christ, that
the glories of Mary are for the sake of Jesus and

that we praise and bless her as the first of creatures,
that we may duly confess him as our sole Creator."

With masterful strokes he fills out and completes
the understanding of Mary. He felt compelled to
hold as an Anglican:

> A mother without a home in the Church, without
> dignity, without gifts, would have been, as far as the
> defence of the Incarnation goes, no mother at all. . .
> why should she have such prerogatives we ask,
> unless he be God? And what must he be by nature,
> when she is so high by grace? This is why she had
> other prerogatives besides, namely, the gifts of
> personal purity and intercessory power, distinct
> from her maternity; she is personally endowed that
> she may perform her office well; she is exalted in
> herself, that she may minister to Christ.

5 AN AGE OF MARY?

The Second Vatican Council noted in its chapter on Mary that the history of the Church shows a certain spontaneity in devotion to the Mother of God.

> From the most ancient times the Blessed Virgin has been venerated under the title "God-bearer" (Theotokos). In all perils and needs the faithful have fled prayerfully to her protection.

This is very true. The Marian devotional tradition in the Catholic Church is very much a product of the instinctive faith of the Christian people. The simple and the unlearned, moved by the Spirit of God, were not slow to recognise in a mother's love the delicacy of the mercy of God. They were strengthened and helped in our own age in particular by the word of the successors of Peter. The final and authoritative recognition of Mary in the Church as immaculate and assumed to glory came from the supreme teacher, the Pope. But the initial insights which started the Church on her way to the discovery of these truths in their fullness were born in the hearts of simple

Christian people under the guidance of the Holy Spirit. The Marian tradition of the Church shows plainly that neither theologian nor bishop has a monopoly of the Holy Spirit, who breathes where he wills *(Jo 3:8)* and who it seems, perhaps particularly in Mary's case, has used the weak things of this world to confound the strong *(1 Cor 1: 27f.)*. It remains true however that the Spirit has strengthened, confirmed, authenticated and purified the faithful's understanding of Mary through the teachers of the Church, particularly through the popes.

In the last century Bernadette of Lourdes stands out as an example of the simple, poor and humble who have always been in a particular way Mary's own. Living at the same time as Bernadette, Pope Pius IX, the pope of the Immaculate Conception, is a clear instance of how the Church's teachers confirm and strengthen the faithful in their devotion to the Mother of God.

Bernadette of Lourdes

> I told what I had seen and heard. If after that people did not want to believe me they were free. That was not my business.

These words of gospel simplicity are words of Bernadette Soubirous spoken in answer to a priest in 1865, about 7 years after the apparitions. From the very beginning Bernadette had to contend

with suspicion, disbelief, threats, deliberate mis-
interpretations, and clerical disapproval, but in
face of all her problems she showed an astonishing
patience, persistence and joy. She refused all
personal gain and wanted no fame from the
strange events of Massabielle.

This interview between civil official Jacomet
and the 14 year old illiterate, who looked about
10 years old, may give us some idea of the quality
of the woman.

Jacomet:	Your name?
Bernadette:	Bernadette.
Jacomet:	Bernadette what?
Bernadette:	Soubirous.
Jacomet:	Your father?
Bernadette:	Francis.
Jacomet:	Your mother?
Bernadette:	Louise.
Jacomet:	Louise what?
Bernadette:	Soubirous.
Jacomet:	I want her former name, her maiden name.
Bernadette:	Casterot.
Jacomet:	Your age?
Bernadette:	13 or 14 years.
Jacomet:	Is it 13 or 14?
Bernadette:	I don't know.
Jacomet:	Can you read or write?
Bernadette:	No, sir.
Jacomet:	Do you not go to school?
Bernadette:	Not often.
Jacomet:	What do you do then?
Bernadette:	I mind my little brothers.

Jacomet:	Do you go to catechism?
Bernadette:	Yes, sir.
Jacomet:	Have you made your First Communion?
Bernadette:	No.
Jacomet:	And yet, Bernadette, you see the Blessed Virgin?
Bernadette:	I did not say I saw the Blessed Virgin.
Jacomet:	Ah good! you saw nothing.
Bernadette:	I saw something.
Jacomet:	Well, what did you see?
Bernadette:	Something white.
Jacomet:	Something or some person?
Bernadette:	It had the form of a little girl.

A brief answer to each question, no more. A simple precise answer.

Fidelity of Bernadette

Bernadette showed absolute fidelity to the directives she was given. She was a very humble person but firm as a rock in trying to see that the wishes of the Lady were carried out. She did not, at any time, insist on understanding all that was going on. Her simplicity and fidelity reflect in a strangely impressive way the qualities of the Immaculate Virgin, whose messenger she was. Her whole life, indeed, from beginning to end and not merely in the time following the apparition, was a reflection of Mary's life and an imitation of Mary's qualities. Bernadette brought a message

of prayer and penance for sin. She lived this
message in her own life and people were struck
by her prayerfulness.

Dutour:	You make the whole world run there. I will have to prevent you, if you keep this up.
Bernadette:	Stop the world from going there. I did not ask them to come. . .
Dutour:	But you — you go there!
Bernadette:	But I have promised . . .

Her fidelity to the Apparition's message and
her religious vocation brought her great suffering
in her life. Yet in spite of all this suffering and
constant ill-health (she was an asthmatic)
Bernadette was joyful and gay. A contemporary
report from the year 1864, the year she became
a nun, says of her:

> She was very exact in following her little daily programme.
> She went to Mass every day and to Holy Communion
> three times a week: Sunday, Wednesday and Friday.
> She visited the Blessed Sacrament every day and recited
> the Rosary. When she prayed one would imagine she
> was in ecstasy, she was so devout and recollected . . .
>
> She always helped when she was asked. She was greatly
> loved by all who knew her. She was a happy fun-
> loving person and loved to tease one of her cousins.

She was a true and faithful witness. Her life, like
Mary's, was a life of faithfulness to God's call.

The Marian piety of Pope Pius IX (1846-78)

Pius IX had a strong personal devotion to the
Mother of God. This comes through very clearly
in his simple address to the Church after he had
defined the dogma of the Immaculate Conception.

Our speech overflows with joy, and our tongue with
exultation. We give and we shall continue to give the
humblest and deepest thanks to Jesus Christ our
Lord because through his singular favour he has
allowed us, unworthy as we are, to decree and offer
this honour and glory and praise to his most Holy
Mother. We have the surest hope and the most utter
confidence that the most Blessed Virgin, who, all
fair and immaculate, has crushed the poisonous head
of the cruel serpent and brought salvation to the world. . .
who is the safest refuge and the most reliable helper of
all who are in danger, and the most influential Mediatrix
and Conciliatrix of the whole world with her only-
begotten Son . . . who has ever destroyed all heresies
and delivered faithful nations and peoples from the
greatest and most varied calamities . . . will through her
most influential patronage graciously bring it about . .
that the guilty obtain pardon, the sick healing, the
weak of heart courage, the afflicted consolation, and
those in danger assistance; and that all who are in
error, may with the removal of all blindness of spirit,
return to the path of truth and justice, and that there
may be one flock and one shepherd.

Let all the children of the Catholic Church who are
most dear to us hear our words, and with even more
ardent zeal for piety, religion and love, continue to
cherish, invoke and beseech the Blessed Virgin Mary,
Mother of God, conceived without original sin, and
let them with entire confidence have recourse to this
sweetest Mother of grace and mercy in all dangers,
difficulties, necessities, doubts and fears. For nothing
need be feared, and nothing need be despaired of, so

long as she is our guide, our patroness, so long as she
is propitious, she our protectress. Surely, she who
through her interest in the affairs of all mankind is
solicitous for our salvation, and who has been
appointed by the Lord as Queen of heaven and earth,
and has been exalted above all the choirs of the angels
and the ranks of the saints, surely she, standing at the
right hand of her only-begotten Son, our Lord Jesus
Christ, and with a mother's prayer, is most influential
in her intercession, and obtains what she asks and
cannot be denied.

A popular Marian movement: The Legion of Mary

The long pontificate of Pope Pius XII saw a
great development of lay apostolic associations
which had placed themselves under Mary's
patronage. It is hardly being chauvinistic to say
that the Irish-founded Legion of Mary was outstanding among these groups as it spread right across the
world from its headquarters in Dublin.

The Holy Spirit is invoked solemnly at the
ceremony of the entry of each new member to
the Legion; he is invoked at the beginning of
every Legion meeting. If the Legion of Mary is
Mary-conscious, this does not appear to prevent
it from being conscious of the role of the Holy
Spirit in the salvation of men. Indeed the hand-
book seems to suggest that those who seek to be
conscious of Mary's role in human salvation will
discover through her the Holy Spirit himself. This
conviction of a bond existing between the Holy
Spirit and Mary in the salvation of men is very
old in the Church. Already in the gospel of St

Luke we see the figure of the Woman over-
shadowed by the Spirit to form "the first-born
among many brothers". This is the pattern of
salvation. We are all to be re-created by the power
of the Spirit in the womb of the mysterious
Mother of all men, the Church our Mother, which
includes Mary. The Legion of Mary has understood clearly this work of the Spirit through
Mary and has sought to promote it. It has had
phenomenal success in this in the fifty years of
its existence.

The future of the Legion

Because its basic theological and spiritual insight
— that the Holy Spirit works to save men in and
through Mary — is sound, one can confidently
predict a future for the Legion which will be even
more rich than its past. But the price of adapt-
ation must be paid and the pain of criticism
undergone. To refuse to change human structures
is to wish for death or to opt for irrelevance. To
refuse to adapt human structures to changing
human circumstances would seem to be a way to
make the Holy Spirit's work less effective.

A question of proportion

The characteristic setting for the Legion meeting
is well known. On the table around which the
meeting takes place we find a statue of the Blessed

Virgin and the Legionary Standard, the Vexillum.
There is no doubt that the focal point of any
meeting is the statue of Mary; it dominates. The
Vexillum appears in its shadow. It might be
preferable and it would certainly express better
the Legion's basic position on Mary's relation
to the Holy Spirit, if the representation of the
Holy Spirit were made to dominate the meeting.
The representation of Mary must appear clearly
and unambiguously as that of a human instrument of the Sanctifying Spirit. She is a human
being infinitely removed from the greatness, glory
and power of God yet nonetheless "the Lord's
servant-girl" even now in the the salvation of
men. Faith demands accurate representation of
what we believe.

"Terrible as an army set in battle array"

   Anyone coming to the Legion now cannot
fail to be struck by the military language it
employs and the entire military ethos which it
presses into the service of Mary. It can be
questioned if this language is any longer acceptable and if this religious style can any longer
be usefully employed to involve people with
Mary in the love and service of God and their
fellow men. To a generation of Christians
aware as perhaps no other generation before in
the history of the Church of the tragic fragility of
man's life, military language is a hangover from
a primitive past. A generation whose aim is peace

must be brought face to face with the Mother
of him who is our Peace. As the epistle to the
Ephesians reminds us: He made us all one and
has broken down the dividing walls of hostility
between men *(cf. Eph 2:14).* Peace was his
word to men. Peace was his life's work. His
death was the price of peace — peace on earth
between men, peace in the acknowledgement
that all men are God's sons. Jesus the son of
Mary is our peace. And so even as we call her
Mother of Mercy so we can call her Mother of
our Peace. The Spirit who works through Mary
is the Spirit of Love and of Life, not of War
and death. Mary is the Mother of Life; the
Mother of Fair Love, of Knowledge, and of Holy
Hope. Military thinking in her regard must become
something of the past. She is the Virgin of
Gentleness, the Queen of Peace.

Legion and charismatic renewal

    The Legionary of Mary is in a particularly
favourable position to welcome and profit from
the new charismatic prayer movement in the
Church. Here the Spirit prays in the hearts of
men, as the Scripture told us he would. In
charismatic prayer groups boys and girls in our
own country have come to an awareness of
Christ in their hearts as a true felt human
experience. It is hard to conceive a charismatic
renewal in the hearts of men which is truly of
the Spirit in which the Blessed Virgin Mary does

not appear. She will be found, in the background
perhaps, but truly there. Charismatic renewal,
aware of the freedom of the Spirit, might learn
from the Legion of Mary the need for structure.
The Legion, on the other hand, might learn from
charismatic renewal the need to possess a human
flexibility. What Mary said was "according to
thy word". She was available to the Spirit, to be
his instrument in God's work of saving man. There
is only one work, only one Spirit who works in
many ways through many different human
realities. These must always be seen as complementary, not as opposed or competing forces.
It is the same one Spirit who works in all and
through all. And he is the Spirit of peace and
concord, the Spirit of brotherliness in the
service of man.

Overshadowed by the Holy Spirit *(cf. Lk 1:35f)*

The evangelist Luke underlines the lowliness
and poverty of Mary by contrast with the greatness and power of God's spirit. And Mary herself
makes this the theme of her *Magnificat.* The Vatican
Council document, *Lumen Gentium,* sensitive to the
Scriptures, also underlines the lowliness of Mary.
In this it may, perhaps, in the providence of God,
be preparing for the emergence of the Holy Spirit
with force and power in the prayer life of the
faithful in the Roman Catholic Church. It may
be that the praise of this generation will be
that praise which will show more clearly than ever
before that Christ is the Lord through his Spirit

and that Mary the Mother of the Lord is the Mother
of Men only in the power of this one sanctifying
Spirit.

Mary: Obscured in our time?

The various forms of piety towards the mother of
God which the Church, within the limits of sound
and orthodox doctrine, has approved according to
the conditions of time and place and the nature and
ingenuity of the faithful, bring it about that while
the mother is honoured, the Son, through whom all
things have their being *(cf. Col 1:15-16)* and in whom
it has pleased the Father that all fullness should dwell
(cf. Col 1:19), is rightly known, loved and glorified
and all his commands are observed.

This most sacred Council deliberately teaches this
Catholic doctrine and at the same time admonishes
all the sons of the Church that the cult, especially the
liturgical cult, of the Blessed Virgin be generously
fostered, and the practices and exercises of piety
recommended by the magisterium of the Church
toward her in the course of centuries be made of great
moment, and those decrees, which have been given
on previous occasions regarding the cult of images
of Christ, the Blessed Virgin and the saints, be religiously
observed. But it earnestly exhorts theologians and
preachers of the divine Word to abstain both from all
false exaggerations as well as from a too great narrow-
ness of mind in considering the singular dignity of the
mother of God. Following the study of Sacred
Scripture, the holy Fathers, the doctors and liturgy of
the Church, and under the guidance of the Church's
magisterium, let them rightly illustrate the offices
and privileges of the Blessed Virgin which always
look to Christ, the source of all truth, sanctity
and piety. Let them assiduously keep away from

whatever, either by word or deed, could lead separated
brethren or any others into error regarding the true
doctrine of the Church. Let the faithful remember
moreover that true devotion consists neither in sterile
or transitory affection, nor in a certain vain credulity,
but proceeds from true faith, by which we are led
to know the excellence of the mother of God, and
we are moved to a filial love towards our mother and
to the imitation of her virtues.

A reading of this quotation from the Second
Vatican Council should be sufficient to dispel
the mistaken impression one sometimes meets
that this Council was in some strange way against
our Lady. Of course it was not. It was against
those things which do no honour to her, such
as pious but misleading exaggerations of her
place in God's plan of salvation, or those caricatures
of devotion to her we find when people forget
that devotion means love and love means
imitation.

No less love and veneration

The Council's love and veneration for God's
mother was no less than that of the great
councils of the past, such as the Council of
Ephesus. Vatican II was very well aware of the
fact that followers of Christ down the centuries
have shown a special sensitiveness and love
towards the human woman who was his mother.
The Fathers of the Council were also aware that
from of old in the Church people approached our
Lady as their mother, and venerated her and
asked her help.

Placed by the grace of God, as God's mother, next to her Son, the exalted above all angels and men, Mary intervened in the mysteries of Christ and is justly honoured under the title of Mother of God, under whose protection the faithful took refuge in all their dangers and necessities. Hence, after the Council of Ephesus the cult of the People of God toward Mary wonderfully increased in veneration and love, in invocation and imitation, according to her own prophetic words: "All generations shall call me blessed, because he that is mighty hath done great things to me" *(Lk 1:48)*. This cult, as it always existed in the Church, although it is altogether singular, differs essentially from the cult of adoration that is offered to the incarnate Word, as well as to the Father and the Holy Spirit.

They commend to Christians today the same love, the same sensitiveness, the same affection for her. They ask them to approach her as their mother. They remind them of the fact that all Mary's power and help is the power of God through Christ. It is not of her own power that she helps us but God helps us through her.

Marialis Cultus places devotion to Mary within
the perspective of the Church's official worship,
the liturgy. The entire first part of the document comes under the heading "Devotion to the
Blessed Virgin Mary in the Liturgy". The Pope
explains with great care that our generation
has seen a tremendously important renewal of
the liturgy and that this renewal is a renewal of
the worship with which the Church "in spirit
and truth adores the Father, the Son and the
Holy Spirit and venerates with special love Mary,
the most holy Mother of God and honours with
religious devotion the memory of the Martyrs
and the other Saints." He stresses that the
liturgy "takes its origin and effectiveness from
Christ, finds its complete expression in Christ and
leads through Christ in the Spirit to the Father",
and is not complete if it does not include some
reference to the Mother of God who was so
closely involved in the salvation of men. Because
of the place which Mary occupies in the plan
of God there is in the Church a special form
of veneration of the Mother of Jesus. Authentic
development in Christian worship necessarily

involves an increase in veneration for the Mother
of the Lord who is our Mother.

When he has set out the abundant and significant material on Mary found in the liturgical
books of the Church, the Pope observes:

> The examination of the revised liturgical books leads
> us to the comforting observation that the postconciliar
> renewal has, as was previously desired by the liturgical
> movement, properly considered the Blessed Virgin in
> the mystery of Christ, and in harmony with tradition
> has recognised the place that belongs to her in Christian
> worship as the Holy Mother of God and the worthy
> Associate of the Redeemer. It could not have been
> otherwise. If one studies the history of Christian worship,
> in fact, one notes that in both the East and the West
> the highest and purest expressions of devotion to the
> Blessed Virgin have sprung from the liturgy or have
> been incorporated into it (15).

The Christological emphasis is constant in the
Church's liturgical veneration of Mary. The Blessed
Virgin is venerated in the Church in the various
Marian solemnities not merely as a helper of the
Christian people by her powerful prayers but also
"as a model of the spiritual attitude with which the
Church celebrates and lives the divine mysteries"
(16).

Mary is not only an example for the whole
Church in worship, but also, as has been long
recognised in the Church, a teacher of the spiritual
life for individual Christians. In her we find
the perfect accord of worship and life which is
the Christian aim. The Christian is drawn to
imitate Mary when he looks on her holiness and
virtues. She is full of grace.

The renewal of devotion to Mary

Piety towards Mary has taken many different forms down the centuries. Time, place, sensibilities of peoples and varied cultural traditions have had part in producing this variety. The local Church today needs therefore:

> to promote a genuine creative activity and at the same time to proceed to a careful revision of expressions and exercises of piety directed towards the Blessed Virgin (24).

What the Pope envisages here in the renewal of Marian devotion is the creation of new forms accommodated to today's needs. He has already referred to the impact which the changes of our time must have on contemporary expressions of "Christian piety in general and devotion to the Blessed Virgin in particular".

> In our time, the changes that have occurred in social behaviour, people's sensibilities, manners of expression in art and letters and in the forms of social communication have also influenced the manifestations of religious sentiment. Certain practices of piety that not long ago seemed suitable for expressing the religious sentiments of individuals and of Christian communities seem today inadequate or unsuitable because they are linked with social and cultural patterns of the past. On the other hand, in many places, people are seeking new ways of expressing the unchangeable relationship of creatures with their Creator, of children with their Father.

Any revision must be "open to the legitimate requests of the people of our own time" (24). Naturally it must also be "respectful of wholesome tradition" (24).

Guidelines for renewal

Popular devotion to Mary must never obscure
the basic trinitarian shape of Christian faith and
worship. If it refers itself constantly to the
renewed liturgy it will escape this pitfall. It must
also be very aware of Christ as its point of
reference. As the document says, "In the Virgin
Mary everything is relative to Christ and
dependent on him" (25). Popular devotion to
Mary must also be keenly aware that all that
Mary does in the Church, and in the life of the
individual Christian, she does as the instrument
of the Holy Spirit. He is the Sanctifier, she is one
human agent through whom he works. Mary
must never be considered either in isolation from
the Church. Her personal salvation history is
prophetic for the whole Church. To love Mary is
to love the Church, for they mirror one another
and mysteriously inexist, the one in the other.

The document emphasises the need for any
Marian renewal to be based on awareness of the
great themes of the Christian message as found in
the Scriptures. The ecumenical concern of the
document is also very obvious (32). *Marialis
Cultus* shows courage and hope in pointing to
the progress which has already been made among
Christians in the understanding of Mary's role
in the Mystery of Christ and the Church, and in
declaring its belief that Mary will become "even
if only slowly, not an obstacle but a path and a
rallying point for the union of all who believe in
Christ " (33).

A new vision of woman and of Mary

   The emancipated woman of today contrasts
rather starkly with the ethereal character and
limited horizons of the Mary of much popular
writing. The Pope declares forcefully the need
to distinguish such socio-culturally determined
presentations of Mary from the simplicities of
the Gospel portrait. He frankly asserts the
incompatibility of certain types of devotional
presentation of Mary with the life-style of today's
self-aware woman. He lists a whole series of
areas in which the traditional woman image has
undergone change — home, politics, employment,
cultural and scientific fields. The horizons of
woman today have grown so wide that they find
it difficult to imagine how Mary of Nazareth, a
woman who apparently lived within very
restricted horizons, can be proposed as an
example to them. Their horizons are the world,
hers the village pump. The Pope suggests that
this is a basic reason why some people today
are becoming disenchanted with devotion to the
Blessed Virgin. He offers some observations which
he hopes may contribute towards a solution to
these problems. He also exhorts the faithful,
local Church leaders and theologians to examine
these difficulties with care. The first observation
the Pope makes it of importance in understanding
devotion to Mary in any age. Mary is proposed
today by the Church as the perfect disciple, the
perfect woman, not in a vain attempt to persuade
woman today to turn her back on the twentieth

century and to adopt the necessarily narrower
socio-cultural horizon of a Jewish girl of two
thousand years ago. The exemplary character of
Mary is to be found in her full and responsible
acceptance of the will of God within her own
limited life:

> She heard the word of God and acted it . . . charity
> and a spirit of service were the driving force of her
> actions. She is worthy of imitation because she was
> the first and the most perfect of Christ's disciples.
> All of this has a permanent and universal exemplary
> value (35).

Christians in the past have spoken about Mary
and related to her in a way which reflected and
was governed by their own view of woman and
her social role. The Church does not feel herself
bound to these past forms. Indeed, she sees
herself called in each new socio-cultural context
to be aware of and to clarify the newer ideas
about woman which are constantly emerging, and
to confront these not with the image of Mary
found in popular writings but with the figure of
the Virgin Mary as presented in the Gospel (37).
If this is done, Mary can be seen to be a figure
relevant to woman today. Mary is a decisive figure,
a figure from whom God asked for an active and
responsible assent. From her was asked a commitment to a future yet to be revealed. In her
personal vocation in the plan of God, Mary's
horizons gradually opened to the limits of the
whole world:

> The figure of the Blessed Virgin does not contradict
> any of the profound expectations of the men and
> women of our time but offers them the perfect

model of the disciple of the Lord: the disciple who
builds up the earthly and temporal city while being
a diligent pilgrim towards the heavenly and eternal
city, the disciple who works for that justice which
sets free the oppressed and for that charity which
assists the needy; but above all the disciple who is the
active witness of that love which builds up Christ in
people's hearts (27).

This generation must test its understanding of
woman with the Woman par excellence whom the
gospels and Christian tradition portray for us.
Mary is not foreign to the modern woman seeking
to share decisively in the shaping of a more human,
more Christian world, for she too was a decisive
woman. Mary's choice of virginity was a response
to a special and unique call. Mary, the prophetic
voice of Israel, spoke long ago for the poor, the
oppressed, the downtrodden — that God would
vindicate them. She herself was a woman who was
poor and humble before the Lord, yet strong in
great suffering. She was the perfect disciple.

Possible deviations in Marian devotion

At the end of the section on popular devotion
to Mary the document offers some words on
possible deviations or weaknesses in popular
Marian devotion, which it is necessary to avoid.
The Second Vatican Council has already indicated
certain things which have no place in Marian
devotion: exaggeration in doctrine or smallmindedness which obscures the figure and mission
of Mary: vain credulity which is associated with

mere externalism in devotion and is backed by
no real commitment to the Christian life. Sterile
ephemeral sentimentality has likewise no place
in Marian devotion. The present document reiter-
ates the conciliar rejection of these distortions
and points out that they cannot be tolerated
because they are not in harmony with the
Catholic faith and therefore can have no place
in Catholic worship and devotion. A more
authentic and vigorous Marian devotion which
will take its inspiration from Scripture
and from solid Church tradition is what is
aimed at. Legends, falsehoods, straining after
novelty or sensationalism must be eliminated (38).
There is one ultimate purpose to Marian
devotion — to glorify God and to lead Christians
to commit themselves to a life which is in
absolute conformity to his will (38). That most
impressive phrase "Blessed rather are those who
hear the word of God and keep it" *(Lk 11:28)*,
which the evangelist places on the lips of Christ
is at one and the same time a word in praise of
Mary, the perfect disciple, and a challenge to
Christians.

After the long treatment of the theological
basis of Marian devotion and its implications the
document takes up two very traditional devotional
practices which are widespread in the Western
Church, the Rosary and the Angelus. This should
not be misunderstood as undesirable archaising,
for the general trend of the document is not
backward looking. It shows no anxiety to
encourage the revival of dead forms. Its attitude,

revealed in several distinct places, is to awaken and sustain creativity:

> It is now up to episcopal conferences, to those in charge of local communities and to the various religious congregations prudently to revise practices and exercises of piety in honour of the Blessed Virgin and to encourage the creative impulse of those who through genuine religious inspiration or pastoral sensitivity wish to establish new forms of piety (40).

The Angelus is given only a little space in the document but its biblical character is emphasised, as is the simplicity of its structure and the fact that it recalls the central mystery of the Christian faith, the Paschal Mystery. For in it we recall the Incarnation of the Son of God . . . and pray that we may be led through his Passion and Cross to the glory of his Resurrection (41).

The renewal of the Rosary

The Rosary is a Gospel-inspired prayer. It is a prayerful reflection on the principal saving events accomplished in Christ for our salvation. The prayer moves from the mysteries of the childhood of Christ through the supreme moments of Passion and Resurrection on to the Pentecostal coming of the Spirit and his effects on Mary and the Church. The Rosary is clearly a Christ-centred prayer. A very important feature of the Rosary which the document stresses (47) is the element of contemplation:

Without this (i.e. contemplation) the Rosary is a body
without a soul and its recitation is in danger of
becoming a mechanical repetition of formulas and of
going counter to the warning of Christ: "And in
praying do not heap up empty phrases as the Gentiles
do; for they think that they will be heard with their
many words" *(Mt 6:7).*

The individual who is praying these prayers
is meditating "on the mysteries of the Lord's
life as seen through the eyes of her who was
closest to the Lord" (47).

The liturgy and the Rosary

The Rosary traditionally allowed the little
man to be associated in the Church's hymn of
praise and universal intercession, the divine
office. Liturgical celebrations and the Rosary
therefore, must not be set in opposition to
one another nor must they be confused. They
are clearly complementary and deal in different
ways, on different planes of reality, with the
salvific events wrought by Christ. The document
draws the following clear picture of the association
and distinction of the liturgy and the Rosary:

Once the pre-eminent value of liturgical rites has been
reaffirmed it will not be difficult to appreciate the
fact that the Rosary is a practice of piety which easily
harmonises with the liturgy. In fact, like the liturgy,
it is of a community nature, draws its inspiration
from Sacred Scripture and is oriented towards the
mystery of Christ. The commemoration in the liturgy
and the contemplative remembrance proper to the
Rosary . . . have as their object the same salvific

events wrought by Christ. The former presents anew, under the veil of signs and operative in a hidden way, the great mysteries of our redemption. The latter by means of devout contemplation, recalls these same mysteries to the mind of the person praying and stimulates the will to draw from them the norms of living. Once this substantial difference has been established, it is not difficult to understand that the Rosary is an exercise of piety that draws its motivating force from the liturgy and leads naturally back to it, if practised in conformity with its original inspiration. It does not however become part of the liturgy. In fact, meditation on the mysteries of the Rosary, by familiarising the hearts and minds of the faithful with the mysteries of Christ, can be an excellent preparation for the celebration of those same mysteries in the liturgical action and can also become a continuing echo thereof (48).

The conclusion of the document contains a summary of the basic ideas on Marian devotion put forward in it. It makes specific mention of the pastoral effectiveness of devotion to the Mother of God and its reality as a force for renewing Christian life. Christ is the only way to the Father but the Church, taught by the Holy Spirit and profiting from centuries of experience, knows that devotion to the Mother, closely linked with the worship of the divine Saviour, has great pastoral effectiveness for the renewal of Christian living. Mary's many-sided mission to the people of God is directed towards producing in the children, her children, the spiritual characteristics of the First-Born Son, Jesus Christ. The Catholic Church endowed with centuries of experience, recognises in devotion to the Blessed Virgin a powerful aid

for man as he strives for his fulfilment which is
to become like Christ.

A final quotation presents an inspiring picture
of the Virgin Mary as the woman to whom man
today can turn in the agony of his unbelief (57).

> Contemplated in the episodes of the Gospels and in
> the reality which she already possesses in the City
> of God, the Blessed Virgin Mary offers a calm vision
> and a reassuring word to modern man, torn as he
> often is between anguish and hope, defeated by the
> sense of his own limitations and assailed by limitless
> aspirations, troubled in his mind and divided in his
> heart, uncertain before the riddle of death, oppressed
> by loneliness while yearning for fellowship, a prey to
> boredom and disgust. She shows forth the victory of
> hope over anguish, of fellowship over solitude, of
> peace over anxiety, of joy and beauty over boredom
> and disgust, of eternal visions over earthly ones, of life
> over death.

PART 2
SELECTIONS FROM MARIAN LITERATURE

HYMN OF PRAISE TO
THE MOTHER OF GOD

Akathistos hymn

Dedication

To thee, protectress, leader of my army,
    victory!
I, thy city, from danger freed,
    this song of thanks
inscribe to thee,
    mother of God.
Since thou hast an unconquerable power,
free me from all danger,
that I may sing to thee:
Hail! mother undefiled!

Preamble

Having understood
    his secret bidding,
quickly the angel went
    into Joseph's hut
and said to the unwedded
    virgin:
"He who bowed heaven to condescension
is closing himself wholly and unchanged within thee.
And seeing how in thy bosom
he is taking the form of a servant
I wonder and cry to thee:
Hail! mother undefiled!"

*The initial letters of the stanzas are the
successive letters of the alphabet*

I

A prince of angels
was sent from heaven
to greet the mother of God,
and upon his unbodied word,
seeing thee, O Lord,
    take body,
he stood in ecstasy and
cried to thee this greeting:

Hail! by whom gladness
    will be enkindled;
hail! by whom the curse
    will be quenched.
Hail! righting
    of the fallen Adam;
hail! ransom
    of Eve's tears.
Hail! height unscaled
    by human reasonings;
hail! depth inscrutable
    even to angel's eyes.
Hail! for thou art
    the king's seat;
hail! for thou bearest him,
    who beareth all.
Hail! thou star
    that makest the sun to shine;

hail! thou womb
   of God's incarnation.
Hail! thou by whom
   all creation is renewed;
hail! thou through whom
   the Creator became a babe.
Hail! mother undefiled!

II

The blessed virgin,
seeing herself chaste,
said unto Gabriel resolutely:
"The contradiction in thy assertion
seems very hard
   to my soul.
Thou foretellest me a childbirth
by seedless conception, and criest:
   Alleluia!"

III

The virgin, yearning to know
the unknowable knowledge,
exclaimed to the servant:
"From my maiden womb
how may a child be born?
   Tell me."
To her he answered
timorously, crying out:
Hail! initiated
   into the unspeakable counsel;
hail! faith
   in what has to remain secret.

Hail! of Christ's wonders
   the beginning;
hail! of all tenets about him
   the summary.
Hail! heavenly ladder
   by which God came down;
hail! bridge that carries
   the earth- born into heaven.
Hail! marvel much spoken of
   by the angels;
hail! wounding most lamentable
   for the demons.
Hail! who mysteriously
   gavest birth to the light;
hail! who the manner
   to none hast taught.
Hail! who outsoarest
   the learning of the wise;
hail! who enlightenest
   the mind of the faithful.
Hail! mother undefiled!

IV

The power from on high
overshadowed then
unto conception the undefiled maid,
and converted her fruitless womb
into a meadow sweet
   to all men,
who sought to reap
salvation by singing thus:
   Alleluia!

V

Having begotten God
in her womb, the virgin
hastened to Elizabeth,
whose child, understanding
straightway her greeting
    rejoiced,
and with stirrings as with songs
praised the mother of God:
Hail! scion of an
    unwithering stem;
hail! estate yielding
    untainted fruit.
Hail! who cultivatest
    the man-loving cultivator,
hail! who plantest
    the planter of our life.
Hail! field which produces
    a harvest of mercies;
hail! board which bearest
    a load of pities.
Hail! thou who deckest with flowers
    a meadow of delights;
hail! thou who preparest
    a harbour for souls.
Hail! acceptable
    incense of prayer;
hail! the whole world's
    redeeming.
Hail! God's goodness
    unto mankind;

hail! man's freedom
   to speak before God.
Hail! mother undefiled!

VI

By a storm
of doubts in his mind
the discreet Joseph was troubled.
He knew thee unwedded
and suspected thee hiddenly fecundated,
   O blameless one!
But having learned that the begetting
was of the Holy Ghost, he said:
   Alleluia!

VII

The shepherds heard the angels
extolling Christ's appearance in flesh,
and running as to a shepherd
they saw him as a lamb
   unspotted,
grazing on Mary's breast,
to whom they carolled, saying:
Hail! mother
   of lamb and shepherd;
hail! fold
   of spiritual sheep.
Hail! defence against
   unseen enemies;

hail! opening of
   the gates of heaven.
Hail! for heaven
   with earth rejoices;
hail! for earth
   with heaven makes chorus.
Hail! the apostles'
   never silent mouth;
hail! the martyrs'
   undaunted strength.
Hail! of faith
   the firm foundation;
hail! of grace
   the shining token.
Hail! by whom
   hell was despoiled;
hail! by whom
   we are clothed with glory.
Hail! mother undefiled!

VIII

When the Magi had seen
the star moving to God
they followed its shining.
Holding it as a torch
they sought by its aid the mighty
   sovereign.
Having reached the unattainable,
they rejoiced, and acclaimed him:
   Alleluia!

IX

The sons of Chaldea saw
in the virgin's hands
him whose hands made men;
and knowing him as the Lord,
even though he took the form of a servant,
    hastened
to worship him with gifts,
and acclaimed the blessed virgin:
Hail! mother
    of the unsetting star;
hail! splendour
    of the mystic day.
Hail! thou who quenchest
    the furnace of error;
hail! thou who enlightenest
    the initiated into the Trinity.
Hail! who drivest from his realm
    the foe of men;
hail! who showest us Christ
    as a man-loving Lord.
Hail! who redeemest
    from pagan rites;
hail! who rescuest
    from filthy deeds.
Hail! who stoppest
    the cult of fire;
hail! who savest
    from passion's flame.
Hail! of the faithful leader
    to wisdom;

hail! gladdening
     all generations.
Hail! mother undefiled!

X

Becoming God-bearing
heralds, the Magi went
back to Babylon.
Accomplishing thy prophecy,
they preached thee as the Christ,
     to everyone,
and left Herod as a fool
unable to sing:
     Alleluia!

XI

Casting upon Egypt
the light of truth,
thou dispellest the darkness of untruth.
For its idols, O Saviour,
unable to meet thy strength,
     fell down;
and those who were freed from them
acclaimed the mother of God:
Hail! thou who raisest
     mankind up;
hail! thou who castest
     demons down.
Hail! thou who hast trodden under foot
     the cheat of lies;

hail! thou who hast confounded
   the fraud of idols.
Hail! sea that drownest
   the spiritual Pharaoh;
hail! rock that waterest
   the thirsting for life.
Hail! column of fire
   guiding in darkness;
hail! refuge for the world
   wider than a cloud.
Hail! food
   superseding the manna;
hail! server
   of hallowed delights.
Hail! land
   of promise;
hail! pouring out
   honey and milk.
Hail! mother undefiled!

XII

Unto Simeon, about
to depart from this
deceitful world,
wast thou brought as a baby,
but he knew thee as the
   perfect God.
Therefore he admired
thy unutterable wisdom, crying out:
   Alleluia!

XX

Every hymn fails when it seeks
to compile the fullness
of thy many mercies.
Were we to bring thee as many odes
as the sands of the sea,
    holy King,
we should do nothing worthy
of what thou hast given
to us who acclaim thee:
    Alleluia!

XXI

As a light-bearing torch
shining upon those in darkness,
we see the holy virgin.
Enkindling an immaterial light
to lead into divine knowledge
    all men,
she, the radiance that enlighteneth the mind,
is praised by this acclaim:
Hail! ray
    of the spiritual sun;
hail! radiance
    of the never-waning light.
Hail! lightning-flash
    illuminating souls;
hail! thunder-clap
    frightening foes.

Hail! for from thee breaketh out
   a manifold splendour;
hail! for from thee gusheth out
   a many-waved stream.
Hail! who realisest
   the type of Siloam's pool;
hail! who cleansest
   the stain of sin.
Hail! bath that cleaneth
   the conscience;
hail! mixing-cup
   that mingleth gladness.
Hail! odour
   of Christ's sweetness;
hail! life
   of mystic banqueting
Hail! mother undefiled!

XXII

Wishing to give mercy
for the ancient debts,
the payer of all men's debts
came himself
to them who were exiled
   from his mercy,
and tearing up the deeds of debt,
he was acclaimed by all:
   Alleluia!

XXIII

Exalting thy childbearing
we all glorify thee, too,
as a living temple, O mother of God,
for in thy womb dwelt he,
who holdeth all in his hand,
    the Lord.
He hallowed thee, he honoured thee,
and taught all to praise thee:
Hail! tabernacle
    of God and the Word;
hail! worthier
    Holy of Holies.
Hail! ark
    gilded by the Spirit;
hail! inexhaustible
    treasury of life.
Hail! venerable diadem
    of pious kings;
hail! worshipful honour
    of holy priests.
Hail! unassailable fortress
    of the Church;
hail! indestructible bulwark
    of the Kingdom.
Hail! thou by whom
    trophies arise;
hail! thou by whom
    foes fall.
Hail! my body's
    healing;

hail! my soul's
    saving.
Hail! mother undefiled!

XXIV

O mother worthy of all praise;
O thou who givest birth to the Word
most holy above all saints!
Accept the present offering,
keep from every hurt
    all of us,
and deliver from coming punishment
those who proclaim in unison:
    Alleluia!

LATIN HYMNS TO MARY

Salve Regina

Hail, holy queen, mother of mercy; hail, our life,
our sweetness and our hope! To you do we cry,
poor banished children of Eve; to you do we send
up our sighs, mourning and weeping in this
valley of tears. Turn then, most gracious advocate,
your eyes of mercy towards us; and after this our
exile show unto us the blessed fruit of your womb,
Jesus. O clement, O loving, O sweet Virgin Mary.

Alma Redemptoris Mater

Loving mother of the Redeemer, open door to
heaven and star of the sea, come quickly to the
aid of your people fallen indeed but striving to
stand again. To nature's astonishment you were
the mother of your holy Creator without ceasing
to be a virgin, and heard from Gabriel that greeting
"Hail". Have pity on us sinners.

Ave Regina Coelorum

Hail, Queen of heaven; hail, mistress of the
angels; hail, root of Jesse; hail, the gate through
which the Light rose over the earth. Rejoice,
Virgin most renowned and of unsurpassed beauty.
Farewell, Lady most comely. Prevail upon
Christ to pity us.

Regina Coeli

Queen of heaven, rejoice, alleluia. The Son whom
it was your privilege to bear, alleluia, has risen
as he said, alleluia.
Pray God for us, alleluia.

Ave Maris Stella

Ave Maris stella,
Dei Mater alma
Atque semper Virgo,
Felix caeli porta.

Sumens illud Ave
Gabrielis ore,
Funda nos in pace,
Mutans Hevae nomen.

Solve vincla reis,
Profer lumen caecis:
Mala nostra pelle,
Bona cuncta posce.

Monstra te esse matrem:
Sumat per te preces,
Qui pro nobis natus,
Tulit esse tuus.

Virgo singularis,
Inter omnes mitis,
Nos culpis solutos,
Mites fac et castos.

Vitam praesta puram,
Iter para tutum:
Ut videntes Jesum,
Semper collaetemur.

Sit laus Deo Patri,
Summo Christo decus,
Spiritui Sancto,
Tribus honor unus.

Amen.

THE POEMS OF BLATHMAC

It is Blathmac son of Cu Brettan son of Congus of the Fir Rois has made this devoted offering to Mary and her Son.

1. Come to me, loving Mary, that I may keen with you your very dear one. Alas that your Son should go to the cross, he who was a great diadem, a beautiful hero.

2. That with you I may beat my two hands for the captivity of your beautiful Son: your womb has conceived Jesus — it has not marred your virginity.

10. Noble is the being who has been born to you! There has been granted to you, Mary, a great gift: Christ, Son of God, the Father in Heaven, him have you borne in Bethlehem.

11. It was manifest, maiden, when you were with your Son in Bethlehem of Juda: an angel of bright fame announces his birth to the shepherds.

12. A star of great size was seen which Balaam, son of Beoir, had prophesied; it was it that guided from the east the three *magi* bearing gifts.

36. A hundred sages cannot tell the number of the miracles of the Son of the living God; for it is to save each person that my famous King has come.

37. Hearing to the deaf (pleasant occasion!), keenness to the eyes of the blind, the lepers making an exchange for a clean body, the lame walking about.

38. Every miserable condition that was brought to him which hand of leech could not cure — they would go home sound; they were not subject to nine-day periods.

39. He would satisfy everyone in a gentle manner while he was curing their misery; he took no payment, demanded no fee.

40. Bestowal of food on every pauper, raiment from him to every naked one; for the Son of the living God has taught that everyone would be the better for (practising?) mercy.

46. Your people seized your Son, Mary; they flogged him. There struck him the green reed and fists across ruddy cheeks.

49. When every outrage was committed against him, when capture was completed, he took his cross upon his back — he did not cease (?) being beaten.

50. When his cross was placed between the two crosses of the condemned ones he was raised (alas!) upon the cross; it was very pitiful.

51. A crown of thorns was placed (this was severe excess) about his beautiful head; nails were driven through his feet, others through his hands.

52. A purple cloak was put about the King by the ignoble assembly; in mockery that was put about him, not from a desire to cover him.

53. The Son of God, the Father! A reed was put in his hand at the end; it was said, clearly to mock him, that he was king of the Jews.

54. They tore from him his pure raiment; beautiful was the body that they stripped; lots were cast without any deception to see who might take his blessed spoils.

55. When they thought thus that Jesus could be approached, Longinus then came to slay him with the spear.

56. The King of the seven holy heavens, when his heart was pierced, wine was spilled upon the pathways, the blood of Christ flowing through his gleaming sides.

201. Beautiful maiden, were a hundred tongues to speak of it they could not recount the extent of your Son's power: the repetition would not achieve completeness.

202. He is the true priest according to the order of Melchisidech; it is he that God, the Father, created a time before the morning-star.

203. It is your Son's body that comes to us when one goes to the Sacrament; the pure wine has been transmuted for us into the blood of the Son of the King.

211. Your Son's name is Alpha and Omega — that this be said is no delusion; its eloquent translation is: he is both the beginning and the end.

212. With certainty is your Son safe and living; Mary, there is no doubt; Jesus himself in his own form has come to confirm it.

213. Now, this was his first appearance; he came to his women-folk; he first fortified the women, he comforted the sad ones.

214. He first came after (his) victory to his apostles on Easter day: he showed his beautiful feet and his pierced hands.

215. On Low Sunday he described (this was no falsehood) the signs of his passion; it is then that he gently removed the doubt from Thomas.

226. Safe is your living Son who has power over the four seasons: winter, spring, bright-visaged summer, autumn with its fruits.

227. It is he who makes heat and cold, the King who dies not by decay; his is dew and mist; he is the true prince of a fair kingdom.

228. It is he who raises wave from strand until it submerges the prows of proud ships; it is he who calms the screech of tempests, who casts a fair calm upon the sea.

229. It is he who raises a great keen wind that breaks a forest from stout roots; it is he who pleasantly represses it so that it troubles not even a tiny pool.

230. It is you and your Son whom we speak about that Balaam of yore had prophesied: there would arise a great star of dignity from Jacob.

231. Jesus is the man who has joyfully arisen in Israel; it is in his name (may you bless it!) that all races have hope.

235. His high renowned Resurrection, thereafter his Ascension, his coming to pass judgment (alas!) on the living and the dead.

236. Alas the coming of hardship — it will utterly crush the great elements. Earth and sky will be ablaze; the smile will be wiped from the face of the seas.

237. This will be a severe shaking; the form of the elements will perish; ocean, sea, and pool will be dry, the beautiful stars will fall from heaven.

238. The mountain will be as high as the hollow; there will be great complaint; the world will be a level expanse so that a single apple might roll across it.

239. Before your noble unblemished Son the angel will sound a good trumpet; there will arise at the sounding every dead one who has been in human shape.

240. It is by your Son — enduring deed! — that many thousands will be struck down into the great fire before the Lord passes judgment on the deeds of all.

ANSELM
Prayer to St Mary (1)
when the mind is weighed down with heaviness

Mary, holy Mary,
among the holy ones the most holy after God.
Mother with virginity to be wondered at,
Virgin with fertility to be cherished,
you bore the Son of the most High,
and brought forth the Saviour of the lost human
    race.
Lady, shining before all others with such sanctity,
pre-eminent with such dignity,
it is very sure that you are not least in power and
    in honour.
Life-bearer, mother of salvation,
shrine of goodness and mercy,
I long to come before you in my misery,
sick with the sickness of vice,
in pain from the wounds of crimes,
putrid with the ulcers of sin . . .

You are blessed above all women,
in purity surpassing the angels,
in goodness overpassing the saints.
Already dying I long to be seen by such kindness,
but I blush before the gaze of such purity.

What I want to ask you, Lady, is
that by a glance from your mercy
you will cure the sickness and ulcers of my sins,
but before you I am confounded
by the smell and foulness of them.
I shudder, Lady, to show you all my foul state,
lest it makes you shudder at the sight of me,
but, alas for me, I cannot be seen any other way . . .

Mary, powerful in goodness, and good in power,
   from whom was born the fount of mercy,
I pray you, do not withhold such true mercy
where you know there is such true misery.
The brightness of your holiness
confounds the darkness of my sins,
but surely you will not blush to feel kindness
towards such a wretch?
If I acknowledge my iniquity,
surely you will not refuse to show kindness?
If my misery is too great to be heard favourably,
surely your mercy will be less than it ought to be?
Lady, before God and before you my sins appear
   vile;
and therefore so much the more do they need
his healing and your help.
Most gentle Lady, heal my weakness,
and you will be taking away the filth that offends
   you.
Most kind Lady, take away my sickness,
and you will not experience the dirt you shudder
   at.
Most dear Lady, do not let what grieves you be,
and there will be nothing to defile your holiness.

Hear me, Lady,
and make whole the soul of a sinner who is your
     servant,
by virtue of the blessed fruit of your womb,
who sits at the right hand of his almighty Father
and is praised and glorified above all for ever.
Amen.

Prayer to St Mary (2)
when the mind is anxious with fear

Virgin venerated throughout the world,
Mother dear to the human race,
Woman, marvel of the angels,
Mary, most holy.
By your blessed virginity you have made all
     integrity sacred,
and by your glorious child-bearing
you have brought salvation to all fruitfulness.
Great Lady,
to you the joyous company of the saints gives
     thanks;
to you the fearful crowd of the accused flee;
and to you, Lady of might and mercy,
I flee, a sinner every way, beyond measure distressed.

Lady, it seems to me as if I were already
before the all-powerful justice of the stern judge
facing the intolerable vehemence of his wrath,
while hanging over me is the enormity of my sins,
and the huge torments they deserve.

Most gentle Lady,
whose intercession should I implore
when I am troubled with horror, and shake with
     fear,
but hers, whose womb embraced
the reconciliation of the world?
Whence should I most surely hope for help quickly
     in need,
but from her whence I know came the world's
     propitiation?
Who can more easily gain pardon for the accused
     by her intercession,
than she who gave milk to him
who justly punishes or mercifully pardons all and
     each one?. . .

When I have sinned against the Son,
I have alienated the mother,
nor can I offend the mother without hurting the
     Son.
What will you do, then, sinner?
Where will you flee?
Who can reconcile me to the Son if the mother is
     my enemy,
or who will make my peace with the mother
if I have angered the Son?
Surely if I have offended you both equally
you will both also be merciful?
So the accused flees from the just God
to the good mother of the merciful God.
The accused finds refuge from the mother he has
     offended
in the good Son of the kind mother.
The accused is carried from one to the other

and throws himself between
the good Son and the good mother.

Dear Lord, spare the servant of your mother;
dear Lady, spare.the servant of your Son.
 Good Son, make your servant's peace with your
     mother;
good mother, reconcile your Son to your servant.
When I throw myself between two
of such unbounded goodness
I shall not fall under the severity of their power.
Good Son, good mother,
do not let me confess this truth about you in vain,
lest I blush for hoping in your goodness.
I love the truth I confess about you,
and I beg for that goodness which I hope for from
     you . . . .

If it is — or rather because it is
that my sin is so great and my faith so small,
so cool my love, so feeble my prayer,
so imperfect my satisfaction,
that I deserve neither the forgiveness of sins
nor the grace of salvation,
for this very reason I ask that in whatever way
you see that my merits are not sufficient for me,
there in your mercy you will not be found wanting.
So I ask you to hear me
by your own merits rather than mine,
so that by the goodness you pour forth
and the power in which you abound,
I may escape the sorrows of damnation which I
     deserve
and enter into the joy of the blessed

to praise you, God,
who are worthy to be praised and exalted for ever.
Amen.

Prayer to St Mary (3)
to ask for her and Christ's love

Mary, great Mary,
most blessed of all Marys,
greatest among all women,
great Lady, great beyond measure,
I long to love you with all my heart,
I want to praise you with my lips,
I desire to venerate you in my understanding,
I love to pray to you from my deepest being,
I commit myself wholly to your protection.

Heart of my soul, stir yourself up as much as ever
    you can
(if you can do anything at all),
and let all that is within me praise the good
    Mary has done,
love the blessing she has received;
wonder at her loftiness, and beseech her kindness;
for I need her defence daily,
and in my need I desire, implore, and beseech it,
and if it is not according to my desire,
at least let it be above, or rather contrary to,
    what I deserve . . .

Mother of the life of my soul,
nurse of the Redeemer of my flesh,
who gave suck to the Saviour of my whole being —
but what am I saying?
My tongue fails me, for my love is not sufficient.
Lady, Lady, I am very anxious to thank you for
    so much,
but I cannot think of anything worthy to say to
    you,
and I am ashamed to offer you anything unworthy.
How can I speak worthily
of the mother of the Creator and Saviour,
by whose sanctity my sins are purged,
by whose integrity incorruptibility is given me,
by whose virginity my soul falls in love with its Lord
and is married to its God.
What can I worthily tell of the mother of my Lord
    and God
by whose fruitfulness I am redeemed from captivity,
by whose child-bearing
I am brought forth from eternal death,
by whose offspring I who was lost am restored,
and led back from my unhappy exile
to my blessed homeland. . .

Mary, I beg you, by that grace
through which the Lord is with you
and you willed to be with him,
let your mercy be with me.
Let love for you always be with me,
and the care of me be always with you.
Let the cry of my need, as long as it persists,
be with you,

and the care of your goodness, as long as I need it,
be with me.
Let joy in your blessedness be always with me,
and compassion for my wretchedness, where I need
    it,
be with you . . .

Blessed assurance, safe refuge,
the mother of God is our mother.
The mother of him in whom alone we have hope,
whom alone we fear,
is our mother.
The mother of him who alone saves and condemns
is our mother.

You are blessed and exalted
not for yourself alone but for us too.
What great and loving thing is this
that I see coming to us through you?

Seeing it I rejoice, and hardly dare to speak of it.
For if you, Lady, are his mother,
surely then your sons are his brothers?
But who are the brothers and of whom?
Shall I speak out of the rejoicing of my heart
or shall I be silent in case it is too high for me to
    mention?
But if I believe and love
why should I not confess it with praise?
So let me speak not out of pride but with thanks-
giving.

For he was born of a mother to take our nature,
and to make us, by restoring our life, sons of his
    mother.
He invites us to confess ourselves his brethren.

So our judge is our brother,
the Saviour of the world is our brother,
and finally our God through Mary is our brother.
With what confidence then ought we to hope,
and thus consoled how can we fear,
when our salvation or damnation hangs on the will
of a good brother and a devoted mother?

With what affection should we love
this brother and this mother,
with what familiarity should we commit
     ourselves to them,
with what security may we flee to them!
For our good brother forgives us when we sin,
and turns away from us what our errors deserve,
he gives us what in penitence we ask.
The good mother prays and beseeches for us,
she asks and pleads that he may hear us favourably.
She pleads with the Son on behalf of the sons,
the only-begotten for the adopted,
the lord for the servants.
The good Son hears the mother on behalf of his
     brothers,
the only-begotten for those he has adopted,
the Lord for those he has set free . . .

So, good Son,
I ask you through the love you have for your
     mother,
that as she truly loves you and you her
you will grant that I may truly love her.
Good mother,
I ask you by the love you have for your Son,

that, as he truly loves you and you him,
you will grant that I may love him truly.
For see, I am asking what it is indeed your will to do,
for why does he not act as my sins deserve
when it is in his power?
Lover and ruler of mankind,
you could love those who accused you even to death,
and can you refuse, when you are asked,
those who love you and your mother?
Mother of our lover who carried him in her womb
and was willing to give him milk at her breast —
are you not able or are you unwilling to grant your
    love
to those who ask it?

So I venerate you both,
as far as my mind is worthy to do so;
I love you both,
as far as my heart is equal to it;
I prefer you both,
as much as my soul can;
and I serve you both,
as far as my flesh may.
And in that let my life be consummated
that for all eternity all my being may sing
"Blessed be the Lord for ever. Amen."

ST BERNARD
Sermon on Luke 1:26-27. Ph 183,70-71

The Virgin's name was Mary *(Lk 1:2 7)* . . .
which means "Star of the Sea", which is a very
fitting name for the Virgin Mother . . .

She is that bright and brilliant star which
stands over the wide boundless sea of life, as a
shining example of a life lived in Christ.

Man, whoever you are, realise that the
turbulence of human life is to be compared to a
passage through stormy seas rather than to a
passage across dry land. Do not take your eyes
off the radiance of this star lest you be overcome
by the tempest. If the stormwinds of temptation
blow, if you are in danger of running aground,
look towards this star, call Mary's name. If you
are tossed around by the waves of pride or
ambition or speaking evil or jealousy, look to the
star, call on Mary. If the bright ship of your mind
is buffeted by anger or avarice or lust, look
towards Mary.

If you are terrified by the enormity of your
sins, put to shame by your consciousness of evil,
frightened by the fear of judgment, and you feel
yourself slipping into the depths of depression

and despair, think of Mary. In danger, in all need, in doubt, think of Mary, call on Mary. Let her name be ever on your lips and never absent from your heart. And that you may benefit from her prayer for you, follow always the example of her life. Following her you will not stray, asking her favour you will not despair. Keeping her before your mind, you will not go wrong. When she supports, you will not fall; when she protects, you will not fear; when she leads, you will not falter; when she is your helper, you will reach your journey's end.

DANTE
The Divine Comedy

Canto XXXIII

"Thou Virgin Mother, daughter of thy Son,
    Humble and high beyond all other creature,
    The limit fixed of the eternal counsel,
Thou art the one who such nobility
    To human nature gave, that its Creator
    Did not disdain to make himself its creature.
Within thy womb rekindled was the love,
    By heat of which in the eternal peace
    After such wise this flower has germinated.
Here unto us thou art a noonday torch
    Of charity, and below there among mortals
    Thou art the living fountain-head of hope.
Lady, thou art so great, and so prevailing,
    That he who wishes grace, nor runs to thee,
    His aspirations without wings would fly.
Not only thy benignity gives succour
    To him who asketh it, but oftentimes
    Forerunneth of its own accord the asking.
In thee compassion is, in thee is pity,
    In thee magnificence; in thee unites
    Whate'er of goodness is in any creature.

Now doth this man, who from the lowest depth
    Of the universe as far as here has seen
    One after one the spiritual lives,
Supplicate thee through grace for so much power
    That with his eyes he may uplift himself
    Higher towards the uttermost salvation.
And I, who never burned for my own seeing
    More than I do for his, all of my prayers
    Proffer to thee, and pray they come not short,
That thou wouldst scatter from him every cloud
    Of his mortality so with thy prayers,
    That the Chief Pleasure be to him displayed.
Still farther do I pray thee, Queen, who canst
    Whate'er thou wilt, that sound thou mayst preserve
    After so great a vision his affections.
Let thy protection conquer human movements;
    See Beatrice and all the blessed ones
    My prayers to second clasp their hands to thee!"

MARTIN LUTHER

See how simply and ordinarily things, which by heavenly standards are great things, are brought about on earth. Here at Nazareth you see a poor young girl, Mary, not regarded at all, taken for one of the least in the town. Nobody knows the mighty miracle she carries in her and she herself is silent.

She leaves Nazareth with her husband Joseph. They have no maid or serving man. Joseph is the head of the household, but a servant too, and Mary is wife and houseworker. They leave their home, perhaps asking their friends to care for it while they are away.

Can you imagine how they were looked down upon in the inns at which they put up on their journey? Yet they deserved to travel in a golden coach with pomp and attendants. There were many women at the time, wives and daughters of the great ones of the world, who lived in luxurious palaces. But the Mother of God, heavy with child, must travel over the fields in the middle of winter. They were despised, and must make way for everyone till they are given

place in a stable, to share with the animals the same
shelter.

The Virgin Mary was praised by Elizabeth,
called blessed, and Mother of God, because she
was told and had believed that all that had been
said by the angel would be fulfilled. She was
not proud because of this praise which no woman
had ever heard before. For it was a unique praise;
no woman is like you! You are superior to
Empress and Queen. To Eve and to Sara. You are
praised as greater than the nobility, wisdom,
holiness of any other woman.

She is not puffed up by this praise, though it
is very great praise; and though it is true praise.
And she is only fifteen years old! She doesn't say
to Elizabeth: "That is not true", as people do
who turn praise aside to be praised the more. She
acknowledges it and in her humility turns to offer
it to the Giver, God. "It is true," she says: "I am
blessed, and am the mother of him who is
Lord of heaven and earth. This is a great glory
and an unspeakable grace and gift. But it is not
my own." She confesses her great and glorious
gift of her honour, and nonetheless she disclaims
it as her own .

She is praised above all virgins and all women
from the beginning of the world, but she despises
no woman. The Holy Spirit teaches the heart to
recognise the greatest gifts without pride, with
humility . . . . "My heart," (Mary says,) "what I
have is from the Lord . . . it is the salvation
of my God. I have not merited or earned it . . .
He has seen that I am a poor girl with nothing.

It is because of his mercy that he wished to look on someone despised like me . . .

(See W. Tappolet, *Das Marienlob der Reformatoren*, Katzmann-Verlag, Tuebingen, 1962.pp 66f.)

THE COLLOQUY OF ERASMUS
The Religious Pilgrimage

Men   Prithee tell me, how does the good man
       St James do?

Ogy   Why truly, not so well as he used to.

Men   What's the matter, is he grown old?

Ogy   You know saints never grow old. No,
       it is this new opinion that has spread
       abroad is the occasion, that he has not
       so many visits as he used to have, and
       those that do come, give him a bare salute,
       and little or nothing else; they say they
       can bestow their money to better purpose
       upon those that want it.

Men   An impious opinion. If this be true, the
       rest of the saints are in danger of coming
       to the same pass.

Ogy   Nay, I can assure you that there is a
       letter handed about, which the Virgin
       Mary herself has written about the matter .

Men   What, Mary?

Ogy   She that is called *Maria a Lapide*.

Men   That's up towards Basil, if I am not mistaken?

Ogy   The very same.

Men   You talk of a very stony saint. But who did
       she write it to?

Ogy   The letter tells you the name.
       I'll recite it to you; but prick up both your
       ears:
       "Mary the mother of Jesus to Glaucoplutus,
       sends greeting. This is to let you know that
       I take it in good part, and you have much
       obliged me, in that you have so strenuously
       followed Luther, and convinced the world
       that it is a thing altogether needless to
       invoke saints. For, before this, I was e'en
       wearied out of my life with the wicked
       importunities of mortals. Everything was
       asked of me, as if my Son was always a child,
       because he is painted so, and at my breast,
       and therefore they take it for granted I have
       him still at my beck, and that he dares not
       deny me anything I ask of him, for fear I
       should deny him the breast when he is thirsty.
       Nay, and they ask such things from me a
       Virgin, that a modest young man scarce dare
       to ask of a bawd, and which I am ashamed
       to commit to writing. A merchant that is
       going a voyage to Spain to get pelf,
       recommends to me the chastity of his kept
       mistress; and a professed nun, having thrown
       away her veil in order to make her escape,
       recommends to me the care of her reputation
       which she at the same time intends to
       prostitute. The wicked soldier, who butchers
       men for money, bawls out to me: 'O blessed
       Virgin, send me rich plunder!' The gamester
       calls out to me to give him good luck, and
       promises I shall go snips with him in what

he shall win; and if the dice don't favour, I
am rail'd at and curs'd, because I would not
be a confederate in his wickedness. The
usurer prays, 'Help me to large interest for
my money', and if I deny 'em anything, they
cry out, I am no Mother of Mercy. And
there is another sort of people, whose
prayers are not properly so wicked, as they
are foolish: the maid prays, 'Mary, give me
a handsome, rich husband'; the wife cries,
'Give me fine children', and the woman with
a child, 'Give me a good delivery'; the old
woman prays to live long without a cough
and thirst, and the doting old man, 'Send
that I may grow young again'; the Philosopher
says, 'Give me the faculty of starting
difficulties never to be resolv'd'; the priest
says, 'Give me a fat benefice'; the bishop
cries out for the saving of his Diocese, and
the mariner for a prosperous voyage; the
magistrate cries out: 'Shew me thy
Son before I die'; the Courtier, that he
may make an effectual Confession, when
at the point of death; the husbandman
calls on me for seasonable rain: and a
farmer's wife to preserve her sheep and
cattle. If I refuse them anything, then
presently I am hard-hearted. If I refer them
to my Son, they cry, 'If you'll but say
the Word, I'm sure he'll do it.' How is it
possible for me, a lone body, a woman,
and a Virgin, to assist sailors, soldiers,
merchants, gamesters, brides and bride-

grooms, women in travail, princes, kings,
and peasants? And what I suffer! But I
am much less troubled with these concerns
now than I have been, for which I would
give you my hearty thanks, if this conveniency
did not bring a great inconveniency along
with it. I have indeed more leisure, but
less honour, and less money. Before, I was
saluted Queen of Heaven, and Lady of the
World; but now there are very few from
whom I hear a Hail Mary. Formerly I was
adorned with jewels and gold, and had
abundance of changes of apparel, I had
presents made of gold and jewels; but now
I have scarce half a vest to cover me, and
that is mouse-eaten too. And my yearly
revenue is scarce enough to keep alive my
poor sexton, who lights me up a little
wax or tallow candle. But all these things
might be borne with, if you did not tell
us, that there were greater things going
forward. They say, you aim at this, to
strip the altars and temples of the saints
everywhere. I advise you to have a care
what you do. For other saints don't want
power to avenge themselves for the wrong
done to them. Peter, being turn'd out of
his Church, can shut the gate of the kingdom
of heaven against you. Paul has a sword.
And St Bartholomew a knife. The monk
William has a coat of mail under his habit,
and a heavy lance too. And how will you
encounter St George on horseback, in his

cuirassier's arms, his sword, and his whinyard?
Nor is Anthony without his weapon, he has
sacred fire; and the rest of them have either
their arms, or their mischiefs, that they can
send out against whom they please. And
as for myself, although I wear no weapons,
you shall not turn me out, unless you turn
my Son out too, whom I hold in my arms.
I won't be pulled away from him. You shall
either throw us both out, or leave us both, unless
you have a mind to have a Church without a
Christ. These things I would have you know, and
consider what answer to give me: for I have the
matter much at heart".

From the Bull *Ineffabilis Deus* of Pope Pius IX
[On the Immaculate Conception of the Blessed
Virgin Mary, 1854]

It is no wonder, therefore, if the pastors of the
Church and the faithful people have made it a
matter to glory in, to profess every day more and
more the doctrine concerning the Immaculate
Conception of the Virgin Mother of God — a
doctrine, according to the judgment of the
Fathers, clearly expressed in the divine Scriptures
and transmitted to us upon the strongest authority,
bearing the impress and sanction of their names,
put forward and publicly adopted in practice, as
is shown by the number of well-known monuments
from times of old worthy of veneration, proposed
to the faithful in accordance with the gravest
and most solemn decision of the Church, and
established with so much piety, religious practice,
and love. So that nothing was to them sweeter,
nothing dearer, than with the most ardent feelings
to honour, to venerate, to invoke, and publicly
proclaim everywhere the Virgin Mother of God
to have been conceived without stain of Original
sin. Wherefore, all along, from times of old, bishops,
ecclesiastics, the religious orders, and even
emperors themselves and kings, have earnestly
implored of this Holy See that the Immaculate

Conception of the most holy Mother of God
might be defined as a dogma of Catholic faith . . .

Wishing to do what was best calculated to bring
the subject in every way to maturity, we established
a special congregation of our venerable brethren
the Cardinals of the holy Roman Church illustrious
for their counsel and knowledge in divinity, and
we have made choice of men, regular and secular,
who were thoroughly trained in theological
learning, that they might with the greatest care
weigh all these points which regard the Immaculate
Conception of the Blessed Virgin Mary, and that
they should most carefully weigh every view, and
lay their special decision before us . . . .

After thoroughly weighing everything with the
greatest diligence, and after pouring forth fervent
prayers to God, we have come to the determination
that there will not be any longer any hesitation
on our part to sanction and define, by our supreme
judgment, the Immaculate Conception of the
glorious Virgin, and this to satisfy the pious
desires of the Catholic world, and our own
devotion towards the most holy Virgin; and at
the same time to contribute, in her person, to the
greater honour of her glorious only-begotten
Son, our Lord Jesus Christ. For to the Son's
glory redounds whatever honour and praise is
bestowed on the Mother.

Wherefore, after we poured forth, in all
humility and with fasting, our own and the public
prayers of the Church, without intermission, to

God the Father through his Son, that he would
be pleased to direct and to confirm our mind
with the strength of the Holy Ghost; and after
having implored the protecting favour of the
whole court of heaven; and having with sighs
petitioned the Paraclete Spirit — and thus while
under his inspiring influence — *We by the*

*authority of our Lord Jesus Christ, of the blessed
Apostles Peter and Paul, and by that invested in
us, do, to the honour of the holy and undivided
Trinity, for the glory and adornment of the
Virgin Mother of God, for the exaltation of the
Catholic faith, and the advancement of the
Christian religion, DECLARE AND PRONOUNCE,
AND DEFINE, that the doctrine which holds
that the Blessed Virgin Mary, in the first instant
of her Conception, has been, by a special grace
and privilege of Almighty God, and in view of
the merits of Jesus Christ, the Saviour of the
human race, preserved and exempted from
every stain of Original Sin, is revealed by God,
and consequently is to be believed firmly and
inviolably by all the faithful.*

From The Encyclical Letter of Pope Pius XII
Mystici Corporis Christi (The Mystical Body of
Christ), 1943

May these our fatherly prayers, which are surely
also yours, Venerable Brethren, find fulfilment,
and all men find a true love for the Church, through
the intercession of the Virgin Mother of God. Her
most holy soul, more than the souls of all God's
creatures together, was filled with the divine Spirit
of Jesus Christ. She, "representing the whole of
humanity," gave her consent to "a spiritual
marriage between the Son of God and human
nature". It was she who gave miraculous birth to
Christ our Lord, adorned already in her virginal
womb with the dignity of Head of the Church,
and so brought forth the source of all heavenly
life; and it was she who presented him, the new-
born Prophet, King and Priest, to those of the
Jews and Gentiles who first came to adore him.
It was in answer to her motherly prayer "in
Cana of Galilee" that her Only-begotten worked
the miracle by which "his disciples believed in
him". She it was who, immune from all sin,
personal or inherited, and ever most closely united
with her Son, offered him on Golgotha to the
Eternal Father together with the holocaust of her
maternal rights and motherly love, like a new

Eve, for all the children of Adam contaminated
through his unhappy fall, and thus she, who was
the mother of our Head according to the flesh,
became by a new title of sorrow and glory
the spiritual mother of all his members. She, too,
it was who by her most powerful intercession
obtained for the new-born Church the prodigious
Pentecostal outpouring of that Spirit of the
divine Redeemer who had already been given on
the Cross. She, finally, true Queen of Martyrs,
by bearing with courageous and confident heart her
immense weight of sorrows, more than all
Christians "filled up those things that are wanting
of the sufferings of Christ for his Body, which is
the Church"; and upon the mystical Body of
Christ, born of the broken Heart of the Saviour,
she bestowed that same motherly care and
fervent love with which she fostered and nurtured
the suckling infant Jesus in the cradle.

May she, therefore, most holy Mother of all
the members of Christ, to whose Immaculate
Heart we have trustingly consecrated all men,
may she who now, resplendent with glory in
body and soul, reigns in heaven with her Son,
use her intercession with him so that from that
august Head abundance of grace may flow with
steady stream into all the members of his mystical
Body. May she now, as in times past, keep watch
and ward over the Church with her most powerful
patronage, and at length obtain from God times
more peaceful for her and for the whole family
of men.

THE LEGIONARY PROMISE

Most Holy Spirit, I, (Name of the Candidate),
Desiring to be enrolled this day as a Legionary of
    Mary,
Yet knowing that of myself I cannot render worthy
    service,
Do ask of thee to come upon me and fill me with
    thyself,
So that my poor acts may be sustained by thy power,
    and become an instrument of thy mighty purposes.

But I know that thou, who has come to regenerate
    the world in Jesus Christ,
Hast not willed to do so except through Mary;
That without her we cannot know or love thee;
That it is by her, and to whom she pleases, when
    she pleases, and in the quantity and manner
    she pleases,
That all thy gifts and virtues and graces are
    administered;
And I realise that the secret of a perfect Legionary
    service
Consists in a complete union with her who is so
    completely united to thee.

So, taking in my hand the Legionary Standard,

which seeks to set before our eyes these things,
I stand before thee as her soldier and her child,
And I so declare my entire dependence on her.
She is the mother of my soul.
Her heart and mine are one;
And from that single heart she speaks again those
    words of old:
"Behold the handmaid of the Lord",
And once again thou comest by her to do great
    things.

Let thy power overshadow me, and come into
    my soul with fire and love.
And make it one with Mary's love and Mary's
    will to save the world;
So that I may be pure in her who was made
    Immaculate by thee;
So that Christ my Lord may likewise grow in me
    through thee;
So that I with her, his mother, may bring him to
the world and to the souls who need him;
So that they and I, the battle won, may reign
with her for ever in the glory of the Blessed
    Trinity.

Confident that thou wilt so receive me, and use
    me, and turn my weakness into strength this
        day,
I take my place in the ranks of the Legion, and
    I venture to promise a faithful service.
I will submit fully to its discipline,
Which binds me to my comrades,
And shapes us to an army,
And keeps our line as on we march with Mary,

To work thy will, to operate thy miracles of grace,
Which will renew the face of the earth,
And establish thy reign, Most Holy Spirit, over
   all.
In the name of the Father, and of the Son, and
   of the Holy Ghost. Amen.

Lumen Gentium

(53) At the message of the angel, the Virgin
Mary received the Word of God in her heart and
in her body, and gave Life to the world. Hence
she is acknowledged and honoured as being
truly the Mother of God and Mother of the
Redeemer. Redeemed in an especially sublime
manner by reason of the merits of her Son, and
united to him by a close and indissoluble
tie, she is endowed with the supreme office
and dignity of being the Mother of the Son of
God. As a result she is also the favourite daughter
of the Father and the temple of the Holy Spirit.
Because of this gift of sublime grace she far
surpasses all other creatures, both in heaven and
on earth. At the same time, however, because she
belongs to the offspring of Adam she is one with
all human beings in their need for salvation. Indeed
she is "clearly the mother of the members of
Christ . . . since she cooperated out of love so
that there might be born in the Church the faithful, who are members of Christ their Head".

Therefore she is also hailed as a pre-eminent and
altogether singular member of the Church, and
as the Church's model and excellent exemplar in
faith and charity. Taught by the Holy Spirit, the
Church honours her with filial affection and piety
as a most beloved mother.

(54) Therefore, as it clarifies Catholic teaching
concerning the Church, in which the divine
Redeemer works salvation, this sacred Synod
intends to describe with diligence the role of
the Blessed Virgin in the mystery of the Incarnate
Word and the Mystical Body. It also wishes to
describe the duties of redeemed mankind towards
the Mother of God, who is mother of Christ and
mother of men, particularly of the faithful. The
Synod does not, however, have it in mind to give
a complete doctrine on Mary, nor does it wish
to decide those questions which have not yet
been fully illuminated by the work of theologians.
Those opinions, therefore, may be lawfully
retained which are freely propounded by schools
of Catholic thought concerning her who occupies
a place in the Church which is the highest
after Christ and yet very close to us.

(55) The sacred Scriptures of both the Old and
the New Testament as well as ancient tradition,
show the role of the Mother of the Saviour in the
economy of salvation in an ever clearer light
and propose it as something to be probed into.
The books of the Old Testament recount the
period of salvation history during which the
coming of Christ into the world was slowly

prepared for. These earliest documents, as they
are read in the Church and are understood in the
light of a further and full revelation, bring the
figure of the woman, Mother of the Redeemer,
into a gradually sharper focus.

When looked at in this way, she is already
prophetically foreshadowed in that victory over
the serpent which was promised to our first parents
after their fall into sin *(cf. Gen 3:15)*. Likewise
she is the Virgin who is to conceive and bear a
son, whose name will be called Emmanuel *(cf.
Is 7:14; Mic 5:2-3; Mt 1:22-23)*. She stands out
among the poor and humble of the Lord, who
confidently await and receive salvation from
him. With her, the exalted Daughter of Sion,
after a long expectation of the promise, the
times were at length fulfilled and the new
dispensation established. All this occurred when
the Son of God took a human nature from her,
that he might in the mysteries of his flesh free man
from sin.

(56) The Father of mercies willed that the
consent of the predestined mother should precede
the Incarnation, so that just as a woman
contributed to death, so also a woman should
contribute to life. This contrast was verified in
outstanding fashion by the Mother of Jesus.
She gave to the world that very Life which
renews all things, and she was enriched by God
with gifts befitting such a role.

It is no wonder then, that the usage prevailed
among the holy Fathers whereby they called the
Mother of God entirely holy and free from all

stain of sin, fashioned by the Holy Spirit into a kind of new substance and new creature. Adorned from the first instant of her conception with the splendours of an entirely unique holiness, the Virgin of Nazareth is, on God's command, greeted by an angel messenger as "full of grace" *(Lk 1:28)*. To the heavenly messenger she replies: "Behold the handmaid of the Lord; be it done to me according to thy word" *(Lk 1:38)*. By thus consenting to the divine utterance, Mary, a daughter of Adam, became the mother of Jesus. Embracing God's saving will with a full heart and impeded by no sin, she devoted herself totally as a handmaid of the Lord to the person and work of her Son. In subordination to him and along with him, by the grace of almighty God she served the mystery of redemption.

Rightly therefore the holy Fathers see her as used by God not merely in a passive way, but as cooperating in the work of human salvation through free faith and obedience. For, as St Irenaeus says, she, "being obedient, became the cause of salvation for herself and for the whole human race". Hence in their preaching not a few of the early Fathers gladly assert with him: "The knot of Eve's disobedience was untied by Mary's obedience. What the virgin Eve bound through her unbelief, Mary loosened by her faith." Comparing Mary with Eve, they call her "the mother of the living" and still more often they say: "death through Eve, life through Mary".

57. This union of the Mother with the Son in the work of salvation was manifested from the time

of Christ's virginal conception up to his death.
It is shown first of all when Mary, arising in haste
to go to visit Elizabeth, was greeted by her as
blessed because of her belief in the promise of
salvation while the precursor leaped with joy
in the womb of his mother *(cf. Lk 1:41-45).*
This association was shown also at the birth of our
Lord, who did not diminish his mother's virginal
integrity but sanctified it, when the Mother of
God joyfully showed her first-born Son to the
shepherds and Magi. When she presented him to
the Lord in the temple, making the offering of the
poor, she heard Simeon foretelling at the same
time that her Son would be a sign of contradiction
and that a sword would pierce the mother's soul,
that out of many hearts thoughts might be
revealed *(cf. Lk 2:34-35).* When the Child Jesus
was lost and they had sought him sorrowing
his parents found him in the temple, taken up
with the things which were his Father's business.
They did not understand the reply of the Son.
But his mother, to be sure, kept all these things
to be pondered over in her heart *(cf. Lk 2:41-51).*

58. In the public life of Jesus, Mary made
significant appearances. This was so even at the
very beginning, when she was moved by pity at
the marriage feast of Cana,.and her intercession
brought about the beginning of miracles by Jesus,
the Messiah *(Jn 2:1-11).* In the course of her
Son's preaching she received his praise when, in
extolling a kingdom beyond the calculations and
bonds of flesh and blood, he declared blessed
(cf. Mk 3:35; Lk 11:27-28), those who heard

and kept the word of God, as she was faithfully doing *(cf. Lk 2:19-51)*. Thus the Blessed Virgin advanced in her pilgrimage of faith, and loyally persevered in her union with her Son unto the cross. There she stood, in keeping with the divine plan *(cf. Jn 19:25)*, suffering grievously with her only-begotten Son. There she united herself with a maternal heart to his sacrifice, and lovingly consented to the immolation of this Victim which she herself had brought forth. Finally, the same Christ Jesus dying on the cross gave her as a mother to his disciple, when he said: "Woman, behold thy son" *(Jn 19:26-27)*.

59. But since it pleased God not to manifest solemnly the mystery of the salvation of the human race until he poured forth the Spirit promised by Christ, we see the apostles before the day of Pentecost "continuing with one mind in prayer with the women and Mary, the Mother of Jesus, and with his brethren" *(Acts 1:14)*. We see Mary prayerfully imploring the gift of the Spirit, who had already overshadowed her in the Annunciation. Finally, preserved free from all guilt of Original Sin, the Immaculate Virgin was taken up body and soul into heavenly glory upon the completion of her earthly sojourn. She was exalted by the Lord as Queen of all, in order that she might be the more thoroughly conformed to her Son, the Lord of lords *(cf. Apoc 19:16)* and the conqueror of sin and death.

60. We have but one Mediator, as we know from the words of the Apostle: "For there is one God,

and one Mediator between God and men, himself
man, Christ Jesus, who gave himself a ransom for
all" *(1 Tim 2: 5-6).* The maternal duty of Mary
towards men in no way obscures or diminishes
this unique mediation of Christ, but rather shows
its power. For all the saving influences of the
Blessed Virgin on men originate, not from some
inner necessity, but from the divine pleasure.
They flow forth from the superabundance of the
merits of Christ, rest on his mediation, depend
entirely on it and draw all their power from it.
In no way do they impede the immediate union
of the faithful with Christ. Rather, they foster
this union.

61. The Blessed Virgin was eternally predestined,
in conjunction with the incarnation of the divine
Word, to be the Mother of God. By decree of
divine Providence, she served on earth as the
loving mother of the divine Redeemer, an associate
of unique nobility, and the Lord's humble handmaid. She conceived, brought forth, and nourished
Christ. She presented him to the Father in the
temple, and was united with him in suffering as
he died on the cross. In an utterly singular way
she cooperated by her obedience, faith, hope and
burning charity in the Saviour's work of restoring
supernatural life to souls. For this reason she is
a mother to us in the order of grace.

62. This maternity of Mary in the order of grace
began with the consent which she gave in faith
at the Annunciation and which she sustained
without wavering beneath the cross. This maternity

will last without interruption until the eternal
fulfilment of all the elect. For, taken up to
heaven, she did not lay aside this saving role, but
by her manifold acts of intercession continues to
win for us gifts of eternal salvation. By her maternal
charity, Mary cares for the brethren of her Son, who
still journey on earth surrounded by dangers and
difficulties, until they are led to their happy
fatherland. Therefore the Blessed Virgin is invoked
by the Church under the titles of Advocate,
Auxiliatrix, Adjutrix, and Mediatrix. These,
however, are to be so understood that they neither
take away from nor add anything to the dignity
and efficacy of Christ, the one Mediator. For no
creature could ever be classed with the Incarnate
Word and Redeemer. But, just as the priesthood
of Christ is shared in various ways both by sacred
ministers and by the faithful and as the one goodness of God is in reality communicated diversely to
his creatures, so also the unique mediation of the
Redeemer does not exclude but rather gives rise
among creatures to a manifold cooperation which
is but a sharing in this unique source. The Church
does not hesitate to profess this subordinate role
of Mary. She experiences it continuously and
commends it to the hearts of the faithful, so that
encouraged by this maternal help they may more
closely adhere to the Mediator and Redeemer.

63. Through the gift and role of divine maternity,
Mary is united with her Son, the Redeemer, and
with his singular graces and offices. By these,
the Blessed Virgin is also intimately united with

the Church. As St Ambrose taught, the Mother of
God is a model of the Church in the matter of faith,
charity, and perfect union with Christ. For in the
mystery of the Church, the blessed Virgin stands out
in eminent and singular fashion as exemplar of both
virginity and motherhood. For, believing and
obeying, Mary brought forth on earth the
Father's Son. This she did, knowing not man but
over-shadowed by the Holy Spirit. She was the
new Eve, who put her absolute trust not in the
ancient serpent but in God's messenger. The Son
whom she brought forth is he whom God placed
as the first-born among many brethren *(cf. Rom
8:29),* namely, the faithful. In their birth and
development she cooperates with a maternal love.

64. The Church, moreover, contemplating Mary's
mysterious sanctity, imitating her charity, and
faithfully fulfilling the Father's will becomes
herself a mother by accepting God's word in
faith. For by her preaching and by baptism she
brings forth to a new and immortal life children
who are conceived of the Holy Spirit and born of
God. The Church herself is a virgin, who keeps
whole and pure the fidelity she has pledged to her
Spouse. Imitating the Mother of her Lord and by
the power of the Holy Spirit, she preserves with
virginal purity an integral faith, a firm hope, and
a sincere charity.

65. In the most holy Virgin the Church has already
reached that perfection whereby she exists without
spot or wrinkle *(cf. Eph 5:27).* Yet the followers
of Christ still strive to increase in holiness by

conquering sin. And so they raise their eyes to
Mary who shines forth to the whole community
of the elect as a model of the virtues. Devotedly
meditating on her and contemplating her in the
light of the Word made man, the Church with
reverence enters more intimately into the supreme
mystery of the Incarnation and becomes ever
increasingly like her Spouse. For Mary figured
profoundly in the history of salvation and in a
certain way unites and mirrors within herself the
central truths of faith. Hence when she is being
preached and venerated, she summons the faithful
to her Son and his sacrifice, and to love for the
Father. Seeking after the glory of Christ, the
Church becomes more like her exalted model,
and continually progresses in faith, hope and
charity, searching out and doing the will of
God in all things. Hence the Church in her
apostolic work also rightly looks to her who brought
forth Christ, conceived by the Holy Spirit and
born of the Virgin, so that through the Church
Christ may be born and grow in the hearts of the
faithful also. The Virgin Mary in her own life lived
an example of that maternal love by which all
should be fittingly animated who cooperate in
the apostolic mission of the Church on behalf of
the rebirth of men.

66. Mary was involved in the mysteries of Christ.
As the most holy Mother of God she was, after
her Son, exalted by divine grace above all angels
and men. Hence the Church appropriately honours
her with special reverence. Indeed, from most
ancient times the Blessed Virgin has been venerated

under the title of "God-bearer". In all perils and needs, the faithful have fled prayerfully to her protection. Especially after the Council of Ephesus the cult of the People of God towards Mary wonderfully increased in veneration and love, in invocation and imitation, according to her own prophetic words: "All generations shall call me blessed; because he who is mighty has done great things for me" *(Lk 1:48)*.

As it has always existed in the Church, this cult is altogether special. Still, it differs essentially from the cult of adoration which is offered to the Incarnate Word, as well as to the Father and Holy Spirit. Yet devotion to Mary is most favourable to this supreme cult. The Church has endorsed many forms of piety towards the Mother of God, provided that they were within the limits of sound and orthodox doctrine. These forms have varied according to the circumstances of time and place and have reflected the diversity of native characteristics and temperament among the faithful. While honouring Christ's Mother, these devotions cause her Son to be rightly known, loved, and glorified, and all his commands observed. Through him all things have their being *(cf Col 1:15-16)* and in him "it has pleased (the eternal Father) that . . . all his fullness should dwell" *(Col 1:19)*.

67. This most holy Synod deliberately teaches this Catholic doctrine. At the same time, it admonishes all the sons of the Church that the cult, especially the liturgical cult, of the Blessed Virgin, be generously fostered. It charges that

practices and exercises of devotion towards her
be treasured as recommended by the teaching
authority of the Church in course of centuries,
and that those decrees issued in earlier times
regarding the veneration of images of Christ,
the Blessed Virgin, and the saints, be religiously
observed.

But this Synod earnestly exhorts theologians
and preachers of the divine word that in treating
of the unique dignity of the Mother of God, they
carefully and equally avoid the falsity of
exaggeration on the one hand, and the excess
of narrow-mindedness on the other. Pursuing the
study of sacred Scripture, the Holy Fathers, the
doctors, and liturgies of the Church, and under
the guidance of the Church's teaching authority,
let them rightly explain the offices and
privileges of the Blessed Virgin which are always
related to Christ, the Source of all truth, sanctity
and piety.

Let them painstakingly guard against any word
or deed which could lead separated brethren or
anyone else into error regarding the true doctrine
of the Church. Let the faithful remember, moreover,
that true devotion consists neither in fruitless and
passing emotion, nor in a certain vain credulity.
Rather, it proceeds from true faith, by which we
are led to know the excellence of the Mother
of God and are moved to a filial love towards our
mother and to the imitation of her virtues.

68. In the bodily and spiritual glory which she
possesses in heaven, the Mother of Jesus continues

in this present world as the image and first flowering
of the Church as it is to be perfected in the world
to come. Likewise, Mary shines forth on earth,
until the day of the Lord shall come *(cf. 2 Pet
3:10),* as a sign of sure hope and solace for the
pilgrim People of God.

69. It gives great joy and comfort to this most holy
Synod that among the separated brethren, too,
there are those who give due honour to the Mother
of our Lord and Saviour. This is especially so
among the Easterners, who with ardent emotion
and devout mind concur in reverencing the Mother
of God, ever Virgin.

Let the entire body of the faithful pour forth
persevering prayer to the Mother of God and
Mother of men. Let them implore that she who
aided the beginnings of the Church by her
prayers may now, exalted as she is in heaven
above all the saints and angels, intercede with
her Son in the fellowship of all the saints. May
she do so until all the peoples of the human
family, whether they are honoured with the
name of Christian or whether they still do not
know their Saviour, are happily gathered together
in peace and harmony into the one People of
God, for the glory of the Most Holy and Undivided
Trinity.

From the Apostolic Exhortation, *Marialis Cultus*
(To honour Mary) of Pope Paul VI, 1974

2. The reform of the Roman liturgy presupposed
a careful restoration of its General Calendar. This
Calendar is arranged in such a way as to give
fitting prominence to the celebration on appropriate
days of the work of salvation. It distributes throughout the year the whole mystery of Christ, from
the Incarnation to the expectation of his return
in glory, and thus makes it possible in a more
organic and closely knit fashion to include the
commemoration of Christ's Mother in the annual
cycle of the mysteries of her Son.

3. For example, during Advent there are many
liturgical references to Mary besides the Solemnity
of 8 December, which is a joint celebration of
the Immaculate Conception of Mary, of the basic
preparation *(cf. Is 11:1-10)* for the coming of the
Saviour and of the happy beginning of the Church
without spot or wrinkle. Such liturgical references
are found especially on the days from 17 to 24
December, and more particularly on the Sunday
before Christmas, which recalls the ancient
prophecies concerning the Virgin Mother and
the Messiah and includes readings from the

Gospel concerning the imminent birth of Christ
and his Precursor.

4. In this way the faithful, living in the liturgy
the spirit of Advent, by thinking about the
inexpressible love with which the Virgin Mother
awaited her Son, are invited to take her as a
model and to prepare themselves to meet the
Saviour who is to come. They must be "vigilant
in prayer and joyful in . . . praise". We would
also remark that the Advent liturgy, by linking
the awaiting of the Messiah and the awaiting of
the glorious return of Christ with the admirable
commemoration of his Mother, presents a happy
balance in worship. This balance can be taken as
a norm for preventing any tendency (as has
happened at times in certain forms of popular
piety) to separate devotion to the Blessed Virgin
from its necessary point of reference — Christ. It
also ensures that this season, as liturgy experts
have noted, should be considered as a time
particularly suited to devotion to the Mother
of the Lord. This is an orientation that we
confirm and which we hope to see accepted and
followed everywhere.

5. The Christmas Season is a prolonged commemoration of the divine, virginal and salvific Motherhood of her whose "inviolate virginity brought the
Saviour into the world". In fact, on the Solemnity
of the Birth of Christ the Church both adores the
Saviour and venerates his glorious Mother. On the
Epiphany, when she celebrates the universal call
to salvation, the Church contemplates the Blessed

Virgin, the true Seat of Wisdom and true Mother
of the King, who presents to the Wise Men for
their adoration the Redeemer of all peoples *(cf.
Mt 2:11).* On the feast of the Holy Family of Jesus,
Mary and Joseph (the Sunday within the octave
of Christmas) the Church meditates with profound
reverence upon the holy life led in the house at
Nazareth by Jesus, the Son of God and Son of
Man, Mary his Mother, and Joseph the just man
(cf. Mt 1:19).

In the revised ordering of the Christian period
it seems to us that the attention of all should be
directed towards the restored Solemnity of Mary
the holy Mother of God. This celebration, placed
on January 1 in conformity with the ancient
indication of the liturgy of the City of Rome,
is meant to commemorate the part played by
Mary in this mystery of salvation. It is meant also
to exalt the singular dignity which this mystery
brings to the "holy Mother . . . through whom
we were found worthy to receive the Author of
Life". It is likewise a fitting occasion for
renewing adoration to the newborn Prince of
Peace, for listening once more to the glad tidings
of the angels *(cf. Lk 2:14),* and for imploring
from God, through the Queen of Peace, the
supreme gift of peace. It is for this reason that,
in the happy concurrence of the Octave of
Christmas and the first day of the year, we have
instituted the World Day of Peace, an occasion
that is gaining increasing support and already
bringing forth fruits of peace in the hearts of many.

6. To the two Solemnities already mentioned (the

Immaculate Conception and the Divine Motherhood) should be added the ancient and venerable
celebrations of 25 March and 15 August.

For the solemnity of the Incarnation of the
Word, in the Roman Calendar the ancient title
— the Annunciation of the Lord — has been
deliberately restored, but the feast was and is a
joint one of Christ and of the Blessed Virgin: of
the Word, who becomes "Son of Mary" *(Mk 6:3)*
and of the Virgin who becomes Mother of God.
With regard to Christ, the East and the West, in
the inexhaustible riches of their liturgies, celebrate this Solemnity as the commemoration of the
salvific "fiat" of the Incarnate Word, who, entering the world, said: "God, here I am! I am coming
to obey your will" *(cf. Heb 10:7; Ps 39: 8-9)*.
They commemorate it as the beginning of the
redemption and of the indissoluble and wedded
union of the divine nature with human nature in
the one Person of the Word. With regard to Mary,
these liturgies celebrate it as a feast of the new
Eve, the obedient and faithful virgin, who with
her generous "fiat" *(cf. Lk 1:38)* became through
the working of the Spirit the Mother of God, but
also the true Mother of the living, and, by
receiving into her womb the one Mediator
(cf. 1 Tim 2:5), became the true Ark of the
Covenant and true Temple of God. These liturgies
celebrate it as a culminating moment in the
salvific dialogue between God and man, and as
a commemoration of the Blessed Virgin's free
consent and cooperation in the plan of redemption.

The Solemnity of 15 August celebrates the

glorious Assumption of Mary into heaven. It is a
feast of her destiny of fullness and blessedness,
of the glorification of her immaculate soul and of
her virginal body, of her perfect configuration to
the Risen Christ; a feast that sets before the
eyes of the Church and of all mankind the image
and the consoling proof of the fulfilment of their
final hope, namely that this full glorification is
the destiny of all those whom Christ has made
his brothers, having "flesh and blood in common
with them" *(Heb 2:14; cf. Gal 4:4).* The Solemnity
of the Assumption is prolonged in the celebration
of the Queenship of the Blessed Virgin Mary,
which occurs seven days later. On this occasion
we contemplate her who, seated beside the King
of Ages, shines forth as Queen and intercedes as
Mother. These four Solemnities, therefore,
mark with the highest liturgical rank the main
dogmatic truths concerning the Handmaid of the
Lord . . .

21. Mary is not only an example for the whole
Church in the exercise of divine worship but is
also, clearly, a teacher of the spiritual life for
individual Christians. The faithful at a very early
date began to look to Mary and to imitate her
in making their lives an act of worship of God
and making their worship a commitment of their
lives. As early as the fourth century, Saint Ambrose,
speaking to the people, expressed the hope that
each of them would have the spirit of Mary in
order to glorify God: "May the heart of Mary be
in each Christian to proclaim the greatness of
the Lord; may her spirit be in everyone to exult

in God." But Mary is above all the example of
the worship that consists in making one's life an
offering to God. This is an ancient and ever new
doctrine that each individual can hear again by
heeding the Church's teaching, but also by
heeding the very voice of the Virgin as she, antici-
pating in herself the wonderful petition of the
Lord's Prayer — "Your will be done" *(Mt 6:10)*.
— replied to God's messenger: "I am the handmaid of the Lord. Let what you have said be
done to me" *(Lk 1:38)*. And Mary's "yes" is for
all Christians a lesson and example of obedience
to the will of the Father, which is the way and
means of one's own sanctification.

22. It is also important to note how the Church
expresses in various effective attitudes of
devotion the many relationships that bind her to
Mary: in profound veneration, when she
reflects on the singular dignity of the Virgin
who, through the action of the Holy Spirit, has
become Mother of the Incarnate Word; in
burning love, when she considers the spiritual
Motherhood of Mary towards all members
of the Mystical Body; in trusting invocation,
when she experiences the intercession of her
Advocate and Helper; in loving service, when
she sees in the humble Handmaid of the Lord
the Queen of mercy and the Mother of grace;
in zealous imitation, when she contemplates
the holiness and virtues of her who is "full of
grace" *(Lk 1:28);* in profound wonder, when
she sees in her, "as in a faultless model, that
which she herself wholly desires and hopes to

be"; in attentive study, when she recognises in
the Associate of the Redeemer, who already
shares fully in the fruits of the Paschal Mystery,
the prophetic fulfilment of her own future,
until the day on which, when she has been purified
of every spot and wrinkle *(cf. Eph 5:27)*, she
will become like a bride arrayed for the bride-
groom, Jesus Christ *(cf. Rev 21:2)*.

25. In the first place it is supremely fitting that
exercises of piety directed towards the Virgin
Mary should clearly express the Trinitarian
and Christological note that is intrinsic and
essential to them. Christian worship in fact is
of itself worship offered to the Father and to the
Son and to the Holy Spirit, or, as the liturgy puts
it, to the Father through Christ in the Spirit.
From this point of view worship is rightly extended,
though in a substantially different way, first
and foremost and in a special manner, to the
Mother of the Lord and then to the saints, in
whom the Church proclaims the Paschal
Mystery, for they have suffered with Christ
and have been glorified with him. In the Virgin
Mary everything is relative to Christ and
dependent upon him. It was with a view to
Christ that God the Father from all eternity chose
her to be the all-holy Mother and adorned her
with gifts of the Spirit granted to no one else.
Certainly genuine Christian piety has never
failed to highlight the indissoluble link and
essential relationship of the Virgin to the Divine
Saviour. Yet it seems to us particularly in

conformity with the spiritual orientation of our
time, which is dominated and absorbed by the
"question of Christ", that in the expressions
of devotion to the Virgin the Christological aspect
should have particular prominence. It likewise seems
to us fitting that these expressions of devotion
should reflect God's plan, which laid down
"with one single decree the origin of Mary and
the Incarnation of the divine Wisdom". This
will without doubt contribute to making piety
towards the Mother of Jesus more solid, and
to making it an effective instrument for
attaining to full "knowledge of the Son of God,
until we become the perfect man, fully mature
with the fullness of Christ himself" *(Eph 4:13)*.
It will also contribute to increasing the worship
due to Christ himself, since, according to the
perennial mind of the Church authoritatively
repeated in our own day, "what is given to the
Mother redounds to the Son . . . and thus what
is given as humble tribute to the Queen becomes
honour rendered to the King".

26. Theological reflection and the liturgy have
noted how the sanctifying intervention of the
Spirit in the Virgin of Nazareth was a culminating
moment of the Spirit's action in the history of
salvation. Thus, for example, some Fathers and
writers of the Church attributed to the work of
the Spirit the original holiness of Mary, who was
as it were "fashioned by the Holy Spirit into a
kind of new substance and new creature".
Reflecting on the Gospel texts — "The Holy

Spirit will come upon you and the power of the
Most High will cover you with his shadow"
(Lk 1:35) and "(Mary) was found to be with
child through the Holy Spirit . . . She has
conceived what is in her by the Holy Spirit "
(Mt 1:18-20) — they saw in the Spirit's intervention an action that consecrated and made
fruitful Mary's virginity and transformed her
into the "Abode of the King" or "Bridal Chamber
of the World", the "Temple" or "Tabernacle of
the Lord" and "Ark of the Covenant" or "the
Ark of Holiness", titles rich in biblical echoes.
Examining more deeply still the mystery of the
Incarnation, they saw in the mysterious relationship between the Spirit and Mary an aspect redolent
of marriage, poetically portrayed by Prudentius:
"The unwed Virgin espoused the Spirit", and
they called her the "Temple of the Holy Spirit",
an expression that emphasises the sacred character
of the Virgin, now the permanent dwelling of
the Spirit of God. Delving deeply into the
doctrine of the Paraclete, they saw that from
him as from a spring there flowed forth the
fullness of grace *(cf. Lk 1:28)* and the abundance of gifts that adorned her. Thus they
attributed to the Spirit the faith, hope and
charity that animated the Virgin's heart, the
strength that sustained her acceptance of the
will of God, and the vigour that upheld her in her
suffering at the foot of the Cross. In Mary's
prophetic canticle *(cf. Lk 1:46-55)* they saw a
special working of the Spirit who had spoken
through the mouths of the Prophets. Considering,

finally, the presence of the Mother of Jesus in
the Upper Room, where the Spirit came down
upon the infant Church *(cf. Acts 1:12-14; 2:1-4),*
they enriched with new developments the ancient
theme of Mary and the Church. Above all they
had recourse to the Virgin's intercession in order
to obtain from the Spirit the capacity for
engendering Christ in their own soul, as is
attested to by Saint Ildephonsus in a prayer of
supplication, amazing in its doctrine and prayerful power: "I beg you, holy Virgin, that I may
have Jesus from the Holy Spirit, by whom you
brought Jesus forth. May my soul receive Jesus
through the Holy Spirit by whom your flesh
conceived Jesus . . . May I love Jesus in the
Holy Spirit in whom you adore Jesus as Lord
and gaze upon him as your Son."

It is our task to exhort everyone, especially those
in the pastoral ministry and also theologians, to
meditate more deeply on the working of the
Holy Spirit in the history of salvation, and to
ensure that Christian spiritual writings give due
prominence to his life-giving action. Such a study
will bring out in particular the hidden relationship between the Spirit of God and the Virgin of
Nazareth, and show the influence they exert on
the Church. From a more profound meditation
on the truths of the faith will flow a more vital
piety . . . .

34. Devotion to the Blessed Virgin must also
pay close attention to certain findings of the
human sciences. This will help to eliminate one of

the causes of the difficulties experienced in
devotion to the Mother of the Lord, namely, the
discrepancy existing between some aspects of this
devotion and modern anthropological discoveries
and the profound changes which have occurred
in the psycho-sociological field in which modern
man lives and works. The picture of the Blessed
Virgin presented in a certain type of devotional
literature cannot easily be reconciled with today's
life style, especially with the way women live
today. In the home, woman's equality and
coresponsibility with man in the running of the
family are being justly recognised by laws and the
evolution of customs. In the sphere of politics
women have in many countries gained a position
in public life equal to that of men. In the social
field women are at work in a whole range of
different employments, getting further away
every day from the restricted surroundings of the
home. In the cultural field new possibilities are
opening up for women in scientific research and
intellectual activities.

In consequence of these phenomena some people
are becoming disenchanted with devotion to the
Blessed Virgin and finding it difficult to take as
an example Mary of Nazareth because the horizons
of her life, so they say, seem rather restricted in
comparison with the vast spheres of activity open
to mankind today. In this regard we exhort
theologians, those responsible for the local
Christian communities and the faithful themselves
to examine these difficulties with due care. At
the same time we wish to take the opportunity

of offering our own contribution to their
solution by making a few observations.

35. First, the Virgin Mary has always been proposed
to the faithful by the Church as an example to be
imitated not precisely in the type of life she led,
and much less for the socio-cultural background in
which she lived and which today scarcely exists
anywhere. She is held up as an example to the
faithful rather for the way in which, in her own
particular life, she fully and responsibly accepted
the will of God *(cf. Lk 1:38)*, because she heard
the word of God and acted on it and because
charity and a spirit of service were the driving
force of her actions. She is worthy of imitation
because she was the first and the most perfect
of Christ's disciples. All of this has a permanent
and universal exemplary value.

36. Secondly, we would like to point out that
the difficulties alluded to above are closely related
to certain aspects of the image of Mary found in
popular writings. They are not connected with the
Gospel image of Mary nor with the doctrinal
data which have been made explicit through a
slow and conscientious process of drawing from
Revelation. It should be considered quite normal
for succeeding generations of Christians in
differing socio-cultural contexts to have expressed
their sentiments about the Mother of Jesus in a
way and manner which reflected their own age.
In contemplating Mary and her mission those
different generations of Christians, looking on
her as the new woman and perfect Christian, found

in her as a virgin, wife and mother the outstanding
type of womanhood and the preeminent exemplar
of life lived in accordance with the gospels and
summing up the most characteristic situations in
the life of a woman. When the Church considers
the long history of Marian devotion she rejoices
at the continuity of the element of cult which it
shows, but she does not bind herself to any
particular expression of an individual cultural
epoch or to the particular anthropological ideas
underlying such expressions. The Church understands that certain outward religious expressions,
while perfectly valid in themselves, may be less
suitable to men and women of different ages and
cultures.

37. Finally, we wish to point out that our own
time, no less than former times, is called upon to
verify its knowledge of reality with the word of
God, and keeping to the matter at present under
consideration, to compare its anthropological
ideas and the problems springing therefrom with
the figure of the Virgin Mary as presented by the
Gospel. The reading of the divine Scriptures,
carried out under the guidance of the Holy Spirit,
and with the discoveries of the human sciences
and the different situations in the world today
being taken into account, will help us to see how
Mary can be considered a mirror of the expectations
of the men and women of our time. Thus, the
modern woman, anxious to participate with
decision-making power in the affairs of the
community, will contemplate with intimate joy
Mary who, taken into dialogue with God, gives

her active and responsible consent, not to the
solution of a contingent problem, but to that
"event of world importance", as the Incarnation
of the Word has been rightly called. The modern
woman will appreciate that Mary's choice of the
state of virginity, which in God's plan prepared
her for the mystery of the Incarnation, was not
a rejection of any of the values of the married
state but a courageous choice which she made in
order to consecrate herself totally to the love of
God. The modern woman will note with pleasant
surprise that Mary of Nazareth, while completely
devoted to the will of God, was far from being
a timidly submissive woman or one whose piety
was repellent to others; on the contrary, she was
a woman who did not hesitate to proclaim that
God vindicates the humble and the oppressed,
and removes the powerful people of this world
from their privileged positions *(cf. Lk 1:51-53)*.
The modern woman will recognise in Mary,
who "stands out among the poor and humble
of the Lord", a woman of strength, who experienced
poverty and suffering, flight and exile *(cf. Mt 2:
13-23)*. These are situations that cannot escape
the attention of those who wish to support, with
the Gospel spirit, the liberating energies of man
and of society. And Mary will appear not as a
mother exclusively concerned with her own
divine Son but rather as a woman whose action
helped to strengthen the apostolic community's
faith in Christ *(cf. Jn 2:1-12)* and whose maternal
role was extended and became universal on
Calvary. These are but examples, but examples

which show clearly that the figure of the Blessed
Virgin does not disillusion any of the profound
expectations of the men and women of our time
but offers them the perfect model of the
disciple of the Lord: the disciple who builds up
the earthly and temporal city while being a
diligent pilgrim towards the heavenly and eternal
city, the disciple who works for that justice which
sets free the oppressed and for that charity which
assists the needy; but above all, the disciple who
is the active witness of that love which builds
up Christ in people's hearts.

38. Having offered these directives, which are
intended to favour the harmonious development
of devotion to the Mother of the Lord, we
consider it opportune to draw attention to
certain attitudes of piety which are incorrect.
The Second Vatican Council has already authoritatively denounced both the exaggeration of content
and form which even falsifies doctrine and likewise the smallmindedness which obscures the
figure and mission of Mary. The Council has also
denounced certain devotional deviations, such as
vain credulity, which substitutes reliance on merely
external practices for serious commitment. Another
deviation is sterile and ephemeral sentimentality
so alien to the spirit of the Gospel that demands
persevering and practical action. We reaffirm the
Council's reprobation of such attitudes and
practices. They are not in harmony with the
Catholic faith and therefore they must have no
place in Catholic worship. Careful defence against

these errors and deviations will render devotion
to the Blessed Virgin more vigorous and more
authentic. It will make this devotion solidly based
with the consequence that study of the sources
of Revelation and attention to the documents of
the Magisterium will prevail over the exaggerated
search for novelties or extraordinary phenomena.
It will ensure that this devotion is objective in its
historical setting, and for this reason everything
that is obviously legendary or false must be
eliminated. It will ensure that this devotion
matches its doctrinal content — hence the necessity
of avoiding a onesided presentation of the figure
of Mary, which by overstressing one element
compromises the over-all picture given by the
Gospel. It will make this devotion clear in its
motivation; hence every unworthy self-interest is
to be carefully banned from the area of what is
sacred.

39. Finally, insofar as it may be necessary we
would like to repeat that the ultimate purpose
of devotion to the Blessed Virgin is to glorify
God and to lead Christians to commit themselves to a life which is in absolute conformity
with his will. When the children of the Church unite
their voices with the voice of the unknown woman in
the Gospel and glorify the Mother of Jesus by
saying to him: "Blessed is the womb that bore
you and the breasts that you sucked" *(Lk 11:
27),* they will be led to ponder the divine
Master's serious reply: "Blessed rather are those
who hear the word of God and keep it!"
(Lk 11:28). While it is true that this reply is in

itself lively praise of Mary, as various Fathers of
the Church interpreted it and the Second
Vatican Council has confirmed, it is also an
admonition to us to live our lives in accordance
with God's commandments. It is also an echo
of other words of the Saviour: "Not every one
who says to me 'Lord, Lord', will enter the
kingdom of heaven, but he who does the will
of my Father who is in heaven" *(Mt 7:21),* and
again: "You are my friends if you do what I
command you" *(Jn 15:14).*

The Angelus

41. What we have to say about the Angelus is
meant to be only a simple but earnest exhortation
to continue its traditional recitation wherever
and whenever possible. The Angelus does not
need to be revised, because of its simple structure,
its biblical character, its historical origin which
links it to the prayer for peace and safety, and
its quasi-liturgical rhythm which sanctifies
different moments during the day, and because
it reminds us of the Paschal Mystery, in which
recalling the Incarnation of the Son of God we
pray that we may be led "through his Passion
and Cross to the glory of his Resurrection".
These factors ensure that the Angelus despite
the passing of centuries retains an unaltered value
and an intact freshness. It is true that certain
customs traditionally linked with the recitation
of the Angelus have disappeared or can

continue only with difficulty in modern life.
But these are marginal elements. The value of
contemplation on the mystery of the Incarnation
of the Word, of the greeting to the Virgin, and
of recourse to her merciful intercession remains
unchanged. And despite the changed conditions
of the times, for the majority of people there
remain unaltered the characteristic periods of
the day — morning, noon and evening — which
mark the periods of the activity and constitute
an invitation to pause in prayer.

The Rosary

42. We wish now, venerable Brothers, to dwell
for a moment on the renewal of the pious practice
which has been called "the compendium of the
entire Gospel": the Rosary. To this our predecessors
have devoted close attention and care. On many
occasions they have recommended its frequent
recitation, encouraged its diffusion, explained its
nature, recognised its suitability for fostering
contemplative prayer — prayer of both praise and
petition — and recalled its intrinsic effectiveness
for promoting Christian life and apostolic commitment.

44. Thus, for instance, the Gospel inspiration of
the Rosary has appeared more clearly: the Rosary
draws from the Gospel the presentation of the
mysteries and its main formulas. As it moves from
the Angel's joyful greeting and the Virgin's
pious assent, the Rosary takes its inspiration from

the Gospel to suggest the attitude with which the
faithful should recite it. In the harmonious
succession of Hail Marys the Rosary puts before
us once more a fundamental mystery of the Gospel
— the Incarnation of the Word, contemplated at
the decisive moment of the Annunciation to
Mary. The Rosary is thus a Gospel prayer, as
pastors and scholars like to define it, more today
perhaps than in the past.

45. It has also been more easily seen how the
orderly and gradual unfolding of the Rosary
reflects the very way in which the Word of
God, mercifully entering into human affairs,
brought about the Redemption. The Rosary
considers in harmonious succession the principal
salvific events accomplished in Christ, from his
virginal conception and the mysteries of his childhood to the culminating moments of the Passover
— the blessed Passion and the glorious Resurrection
— and to the effects of this on the infant Church
on the day of Pentecost, and on the Virgin Mary
when at the end of her earthly life she was
assumed body and soul into her heavenly home.
It has also been observed that the division of
the mysteries of the Rosary into three parts not
only adheres strictly to the chronological order
of the facts but above all reflects the plan of the
original proclamation of the faith and sets forth
once more the mystery of Christ in the very
way in which it is seen by Saint Paul in the celebrated "hymn" of the Letter to the Philippians
— kenosis, death and exaltation *(2:6-11)*.

46. As a Gospel prayer, centred on the mystery
of the redemptive Incarnation, the Rosary is
therefore a prayer with a clearly Christological
orientation. Its most characteristic element, in
fact, the litany-like succession of Hail Marys,
becomes in itself an unceasing praise of Christ,
who is the ultimate object both of the Angel's
announcement and of the greeting of the Mother
of John the Baptist: "Blessed is the fruit of your
womb" *(Lk 1:42)*. We would go further and say
that the succession of Hail Marys constitutes
the wrap on which is woven the contemplation
of the mysteries. The Jesus that each Hail Mary
recalls is the same Jesus whom the succession
of the mysteries proposes to us — now as the
Son of God, now as the son of the Virgin — at
his birth in a stable at Bethlehem, at his presentation
by his Mother in the Temple, as a youth full of
zeal for his Father's affairs, as the Redeemer
in agony in the garden, scourged and crowned
with thorns, carrying the Cross and dying on
Calvary; risen from the dead and ascended to the
glory of the Father to send forth the gift of the
Spirit. As is well known, at one time there was a
custom, still preserved in certain places, of
adding to the name of Jesus in each Hail Mary a
reference to the mystery being contemplated.
And this was done precisely in order to help contemplation and to make the mind and the voice act in
unison.

47. There has also been felt with greater urgency
the need to point out once more the importance
of a further essential element in the Rosary, in

addition to the value of the elements of praise
and petition, namely the element of contemplation.
Without this the Rosary is a body without a soul,
and its recitation is in danger of becoming a
mechanical repetition of formulas and of going
counter to the warning of Christ: "And in praying
do not heap up empty phrases as the Gentiles
do; for they think that they will be heard for
their many words" *(Mt 6: 7)*. By its nature
the recitation of the Rosary calls for a quiet
rhythm and a lingering pace, helping the
individual to meditate on the mysteries of the
Lord's life as seen through the eyes of her who
was closest to the Lord. In this way the
unfathomable riches of these mysteries are
unfolded.

48. Finally, as a result of modern reflection the
relationships between the liturgy and the Rosary
have been more clearly understood. On the one
hand it has been emphasised that the Rosary is
as it were a branch sprung from the ancient
trunk of the Christian liturgy, the Psalter of the
Blessed Virgin whereby the humble were associated in the Church's hymn of praise and universal
intercession. On the other hand it has been noted
that this development occurred at a time — the
last period of the Middle Ages — when the
liturgical spirit was in decline and the faithful
were turning from the liturgy towards a
devotion to Christ's humanity and to the
Blessed Virgin Mary, a devotion favouring a certain
external sentiment of piety. Not many years ago
some people began to express the desire to see the

Rosary included among the rites of the liturgy,
while other people, anxious to avoid repetition
of former pastoral mistakes, unjustifiably dis-
regarded the Rosary. Today the problem can
easily be solved in the light of the principles of
the Constitution *Sacrosanctum Concilium.*
Liturgical celebration and the pious practice
of the Rosary must be neither set in opposition
to one another nor considered as being
identical. The more an expression of prayer
preserves its own true nature and individual
characteristics the more fruitful it becomes.
Once the preeminent value of liturgical rites has
been reaffirmed it will not be difficult to
appreciate the fact that the Rosary is a practice
of piety which easily harmonises with the liturgy.
In fact, like the liturgy, it is of a community
nature, draws its inspiration from Sacred Scripture
and is oriented towards the mystery of Christ.
The commemoration in the liturgy and the contemplative remembrance proper to the Rosary,
although existing on essentially different planes
of reality, have as their object the same salvific
events wrought by Christ. The former presents
anew, under the veil of signs and operative in a
hidden way, the great mysteries of our redemption. The latter, by means of devout contemplation,
recalls these same mysteries to the mind of the
person praying and stimulates the will to draw
from them the norms of living. Once this substantial difference has been established, it is not
difficult to understand that the Rosary is an
exercise of piety that draws its motivating force

from the liturgy and leads naturally back to it,
if practised in conformity with its original
inspiration. It does not however become part of
the liturgy. In fact meditation on the mysteries
of the Rosary, by familiarising the hearts and
minds of the faithful with the mysteries of Christ,
can be an excellent preparation for the celebration
of those same mysteries in the liturgical action
and can also become a continuing echo thereof.
However, it is a mistake to recite the Rosary
during the celebration of the liturgy, though
unfortunately this practice still persists here and
there .

57. Christ is the only way to the Father *(cf. Jn
14:4-11)*, and the ultimate example to whom
the disciple must conform his own conduct
(cf. Jn 13:15), to the extent of sharing Christ's
sentiments *(cf. Phil 2:5)*, living his life and
possessing his Spirit *(cf. Gal 2:20; Rom 8:10-11)*.
The Church has always taught this and nothing
in pastoral activity should obscure this doctrine.
But the Church, taught by the Holy Spirit and
benefiting from centuries of experience,
recognises that devotion to the Blessed Virgin,
subordinated to worship of the divine Saviour
and in connection with it, also has a great
pastoral effectiveness and constitutes a force
for renewing Christian living. It is easy to see
the reason for this effectiveness. Mary's many-
sided mission to the People of God is a supernatural reality which operates and bears fruit
within the body of the Church. One finds cause
for joy in considering the different aspects of

this mission, and seeing how each of these
aspects with its individual effectiveness is
directed towards the same end, namely, producing
in the children the spiritual characteristics of
the Firstborn Son. The Virgin's maternal intercession, her exemplary holiness and the divine
grace which is in her become for the human race
a reason for divine hope.

The Blessed Virgin's role as Mother leads the
People of God to turn with filial confidence to
her who is ever ready to listen with a mother's
affection and efficacious assistance. Thus the
People of God have learned to call on her as the
Consoler of the Afflicted, the Health of the Sick,
the Refuge of Sinners, that they may find
comfort in tribulation, relief in sickness and
liberating strength in guilt. For she, who is free
from sin, leads her children to combat sin with
energy and resoluteness. This liberation from
sin and evil *(cf. Mt 6:13)* it must be repeated
is the necessary premise for any renewal of
Christian living.

The Blessed Virgin's exemplary holiness encour-
ages the faithful to "raise their eyes to Mary who
shines forth before the whole community of the
elect as a model of the virtues". It is a question of
solid, evangelical virtues: faith and the docile
acceptance of the Word of God *(cf. Lk 1:26-38,
1:45, 11:27-28: Jn 2:5);* generous obedience
(cf. Lk 1:38); genuine humility *(cf. Lk 1:48);*
solicitous charity *(cf.Lk 1:39-56);* profound wisdom *(cf. Lk 1:29,34; 2:19,33,51)* worship of God
manifested in alacrity in the fulfilment of religious

duties *(cf. Lk 2:21-41)*, in gratitude for gifts
received *(cf. Lk 1:46-49)*, in her offering in the
Temple *(cf. Lk 2:22-24)* and in her prayer in the
midst of the apostolic community *(cf. Acts
1:12-14)*; her fortitude in exile *(cf. Mt 2:13-23)*
and in suffering *(cf. Lk 2:34-35; 2:49; Jn 19:25)*;
her poverty reflecting dignity and trust in God
(cf. Lk 1:48; 2:24); her attentive care for her Son,
from his humble birth to the ignominy of the
Cross *(cf. Lk.2:1-7; Jn 19:25-27)*; her delicate
forethought *(cf. Jn 2:1-11)*; her virginal purity
(cf. Mt 1:18-25; Lk 1:26-38); her strong and
chaste married love. These virtues of the Mother
will also adorn her children who steadfastly study
her example in order to reflect it in their own
lives. And this progress in virtue will appear as the
consequence and the already mature fruit of that
pastoral zeal which springs from devotion to the
Blessed Virgin.

Devotion to the Mother of the Lord becomes
for the faithful an opportunity for growing in
divine grace, and this is the ultimate aim of all
pastoral activity. For it is impossible to honour
her who is "full of grace" *(Lk 1:28)* without
thereby honouring in oneself the state of grace,
which is friendship with God, communion with
him and the indwelling of the Holy Spirit. It is
this divine grace which takes possession of the
whole man and conforms him to the image of the
Son of God *(cf. Rom 8:29; Col 1:18)*. The
Catholic Church, endowed with centuries of
experience, recognises in devotion to the

Blessed Virgin a powerful aid for man as he
strives for fulfilment. Mary, the New Woman,
stands at the side of Christ, the New Man,
within whose mystery the mystery of man alone
finds true light; she is given to us as a pledge
and guarantee that God's Plan in Christ for the
salvation of the whole man has already achieved
realisation in a creature: in her. Contemplated
in the episodes of the Gospels and in the
reality which she already possesses in the City
of God, the Blessed Virgin Mary offers a calm
vision and a reassuring word to modern man. . .
She shows forth the victory of hope over anguish,
of fellowship over solitude, of peace over anxiety,
of joy and beauty over boredom and disgust, of
eternal visions over earthly ones, of life over
death.

SUGGESTED FURTHER READING

Commentary on the Marian chapter of the Dogmatic Constitution on the Church by Donal Flanagan, in the book edited by Kevin McNamara *Vatican II: The Constitution on the Church* Franciscan Herald Press, Chicago, 1968.

Prayers and Devotions from Pope John XXIII edited by J.B. Donnelly, Doubleday Image Paperback, Garden City, NY, 1969.

F.M. Braun, O.P. *Mother of God's People* Alba House, Staten Island, NY, 1967.

Raymond E. Brown, S.S. *The Virginal Conception and Bodily Resurrection of Jesus* Paulist Press, NY, 1973, Paperback.

Lucien Deiss, C.S.Sp. *Daughter of Sion* Liturgical Press, Collegeville, Minn., 1972.

A. Gelin, S.S. *The Poor of Yahweh* Liturgical Press, Collegeville, Minn., 1967. Paperback.

Henri de Lubac, S.J. *Splendour of the Church* Paulist Press, NY, 1963. Paperback: chapter, The Church and Our Lady, also the pages on Our Lady in Lumen Gentium and the Fathers, in his book *The Church: Paradox and Mystery* Alba House, Staten Island, NY.

Heiko Oberman *The Virgin Mary in Evangelical Perspective* with preface by Thomas F. O'Meara O.P. Fortress Press, Philadelphia, 1971. A Facet Paperback.

Karl Rahner, S.J. *Mary, Mother of the Lord* Herder and Herder, NY, 1963. Reprinted 1974.

Joseph Ratzinger *Introduction to Christianity* Herder and Herder, NY, 1970: chapter Conceived by the Holy Ghost, born of the Virgin Mary.

Edward Schillebeeckx, O.P. *Mary, Mother of the Redemption* Sheed and Ward, NY, 1965.

Max Thurian *Mary, Mother of the Lord, Figure of the Church* Faith Press, 7 Tufton Street, London SWI.

Behold your Mother. A Pastoral letter on the Blessed Virgin Mary issued by the United States Conference of Catholic Bishops, November 21, 1973.

H. Graef *Mary, a History of Doctrine and Devotion.* 2 vols. Sheed and Ward, London, 1963 (Vol 1); 1965 (Vol.2).

T. O'Meara *Mary in Protestant and Catholic Theology* Sheed and Ward, NY 1966.

E.L. Mascall *The Blessed Virgin Mary* Darton, Longman & Todd, London, 1963.

R. Laurentin *Mary's Place in the Church* Burns Oates, London, 1965.

Y. Congar *Christ, Our Lady and the Church* Longmans, London, 1957. (Eng. tr.)

P. Palmer *Mary in the Documents of the Church* Burns Oates, London, 1953.

J. Neville Ward *Five for Sorrow, Ten for Joy* Epworth Press, London, 1971.

G.G. Meersseman, O.P. (ed.) *The Akathistos Hymn* University Press, Fribourg, Switzerland, 1958.

James Carney *The Poems of Blathmac, Son of Cu Brethan* Irish Texts Society Series, Vol 47, Dublin, 1964, p.3, vv 1-3.

J. Pelikan (ed.) *Luther's Works* (tr.). Concordia Publishing House, St Louis, USA, 1956.f. Vol.21.

L.J. Suenens *Theology of the Apostolate* Mércier Press, Cork, 1955.

J.H. Newman *Certain Difficulties felt by Anglicans in Catholic Teaching Considered* 2 vols., London, 1891. (Vol.2.)

Benedicta Ward, S.L.G. (tr.) *The Prayers and Meditations of Saint Anselm* Penguin Books, Harmondsworth, Middlesex, England, 1973.